Day of the Dragon

How current events have set the stage
for America's prophetic transformation.
The *Great Controversy* vindicated.

Clifford Goldstein

Pacific Press Publishing Association
Boise, Idaho
Oshawa, Ontario, Canada

Edited by Marvin Moore
Designed by Tim Larson
Cover art by Darrel Tank
Typeset in 10/12 Century Schoolbook

Library of Congress Cataloging-in-Publication Data:
Goldstein, Clifford.
    Day of the dragon : how current events have set the stage
for America's prophetic destiny : The Great Controversy vindicated / Clifford Goldstein.
         p.   cm.
    Includes bibliographical references.
    ISBN 0-8163-1148-X
    1. Seventh-day Adventists—Apologetic works. 2. Advent-
ists—Apologetic works. 3. White, Ellen Gould Harmon, 1827-
1915. Great controversy between Christ and Satan during
the Christian dispensation. 4. United States—History—Prophecies. 5. Twentieth century—Forecasts.   I. Title.
BX6154.G62 1993
230'.16732—dc20   92-41909
                                                         CIP

93 94 95 96 97 • 5 4 3 2 1

Contents

For K. D.

Other books by Clifford Goldstein:

The Saving of America
1844 Made Simple
Best Seller
How Dare You Judge Us, God?
False Balances
A Pause for Peace

ONE:

The Coming
Great Controversy
Embarrassment

Translated into dozens of languages, printed by the millions, and read everywhere from plush penthouses in Manhattan to thatch huts in Africa, Ellen White's *The Great Controversy* has epitomized the Adventist mission, message, and purpose unlike any work outside of Scripture itself.

Yet today the book's an embarrassment. Look at these references:

God's word has given warning of the impending danger; let this be unheeded, and the Protestant world will learn what the purposes of Rome really are, only when it is too late to escape the snare. She is silently growing into power. Her doctrines are exerting their influence in legislative halls, in the churches, and in the hearts of men. She is piling up her lofty and massive structures in the secret recesses of which her former persecutions will be repeated.[1]

The Roman church is far-reaching in her plans and modes of operation. She is employing every device to extend her influence and increase her power in preparation for a fierce and determined conflict to regain control of the world, to re-establish persecution, and to undo all that Protestantism has done.[2]

Who believes like this anymore? Her words sound like right-wing nineteenth-century fundamentalism. With few exceptions, the only ones who hold these views are the ultra-right Protestant fringe, kooks who believe that blacks have the mark of Cain and Jews are children of the devil. Rampant anti-Catholicism hasn't been part of Protestantism for decades. Words like *Romanists, papists*, and *popery* went out with the Edsel. Today, even the Ku Klux Klan, founded partially on anti-Catholicism, accepts Catholics as members, which means that Adventists print a book that sounds more bigoted than David Duke in his glory days as a Grand Dragon.

When Roman Catholics make up the largest percentage of senators and congressmen in Washington, D.C.[3]; when Catholics are accepted in every aspect of American society, and when the pope is an honored guest at the White House—is this the time for Adventists to distribute a book saying that "every principle of the papacy that existed in past ages exists today. The doctrines devised in the darkest ages are still held. . . . Her spirit is no less cruel and despotic now than when she crushed out human liberty and slew the saints of the Most High"[4]?

When the president of the United States refers to John Paul II as the "holy father," we push a book naming him as the biblical man of sin?[5] When Catholics have been leaders in the anti-abortion movement, when Catholic hospitals refuse to perform abortions, how can Adventists (whose record in that area has been spotty) warn in *The Great Controversy* that Rome's "claim to the right to pardon leads the Romanist[s] to feel *at liberty to sin*; and the ordinance of confession, without which her pardon is not granted, tends also *to give license to evil*"[6]?

Imagine "60 Minutes" doing a segment called "What Seventh-day Adventists Believe." Mike Wallace begins by reading such choice quotes from *The Great Controversy* as, "If we desire to understand the determined cruelty of Satan, manifested for hundreds of years, not among those who never heard of God, but in the very heart of Christendom, we have only to look at the history of Romanism"[7]—*and then the camera dissolves into a shot of Mother Teresa opening an AIDS hospice in New York?*

At a time when John Paul II, one of the world's most respected men, has stated that "no human authority has the right to interfere with a person's conscience" and that "a serious threat is posed by intolerance, which manifests itself in the denial of freedom of conscience to others,"[8] Adventists sell, by the millions, a book warning that the Roman Church is a "most dangerous foe to civil and religious liberty"[9]?

When *The Great Controversy* is displayed before the world, especially when choice quotes are taken out of context, Adventists will look like bigots and buffoons. We've always warned about the shaking, and most think it will be over theology or persecution, but many Adventists will be embarrassed out of the message instead.

What's the point? Why do these statements in *The Great Controversy* seem so outdated, so out of touch with reality, and so far removed from modern thought?

Because they have all come true!

If the majority of Protestants still looked at the Catholic Church as they did when Ellen White wrote *The Great Controversy*, the book would be wrong, its predictions false. But because almost nobody holds such views anymore, the book is proven right. The "embarrassment," "bigotry," and "obsolescence" of Ellen White's words, far from discrediting them, validate them instead. The trends that make the book seem so outlandish actually confirm every page!

Indeed, *The Great Controversy* is more pertinent, relevant, and crucial now than when scribbled out by the wrinkled right hand of Sister White more than a century ago. Despite attempts by some to dismiss *The Great Controversy* as nothing but Ellen White's "eschatological perspective for her time,"[10] the political and religious trends of the past few years have reignited fire into its pages until they burn brighter now than at any time since A. T. Jones battled Sunday-law legislation in Congress.

If you have been reading, studying, seeking to understand the signs of the times, you should see how *The Great Controversy* has assumed unbelievable relevance. The collapse of Communism, the rise of the papacy, the New Right of the 1990s, the conservative thrust of the Supreme Court, the guises of modern spiritualism, the political merging of Catholics and Protestants—these are all pieces of a puzzle reproducing the prophetic picture warned about in *The Great Controversy*.

How *do* these trends reflect *The Great Controversy*? What do they mean? How do they fit our prophetic scenario? How do we safely interpret current events without making the mistakes that have embarrassed Adventists in the past? And what do these events tell us about the timing of the second coming of Christ?

Despite ample opportunity to prepare for the final crisis, many Adventists will be driven away by the coming *Great Controversy* embarrassment. For others, those with a "love of the truth" (2 Thessalonians 2:10), that which pushes out the unfaithful will draw the faithful closer to the One whose Spirit inspired *The Great Controversy* and whose blood has sealed its every page.

The Great Controversy will, no doubt, unleash a storm of persecution against us. Why? Because the dragon makes war against those who, among other things, have the "testimony of Jesus" (Revelation 12:17). And, as worldwide trends confirm more and more every day, that "testimony" is, indeed, "the Spirit of prophecy" (Revelation 19:10).

---

1. Ellen G. White, *The Great Controversy* (Mountain View, Calif.: Pacific Press, 1950), 581.

2. Ibid., 565, 566.

3. "Roman Catholics Lead Affiliation Count in 102nd Congress," *Church and State*, January 1991, 14.

4. *The Great Controversy*, 571.

5. See ibid.

6. Ibid., 567, emphasis supplied.

7. Ibid., 570.

8. *Message of His Holiness Pope John Paul II for the Celebration of the World Day of Peace*, 1 Jan. 1991.

9. *The Great Controversy*, 566.

10. Jonathan Butler, "The World of E. G. White and the End of the World," *Spectrum*, August 1979, 12.

TWO:

New World Order

After an incredible born-again experience,[1] I joined the Adventist Church in the spring of 1980. Having accepted everything—state of the dead, divinity of Christ, second coming, Sabbath, investigative judgment—I was, from day one, hard-core SDA.

What particularly excited me was prophecy, and it was immediately clear how the Adventist prophetic scenario could unfold. First introduced to Revelation 13 and 14 in 1979 during newly installed Pope John Paul II's historic tour of the United States,[2] I saw from the start how trends were moving toward the fulfillment of the third angel's message.

I can remember, however, when still a new believer, I felt overwhelmed with doubt about an aspect of our prophetic message.

What about the Soviet Union?

How could our prophetic message ever happen as long as the world faced the guns, tanks, barbed wire, and walls of militant, atheistic Soviet Communism? How could the United States, much less the Roman Catholic Church, ever wield the kind of international power depicted in Revelation and interpreted in *The Great Controversy* as long as the Soviet Union—a highly aggressive superpower implacably hostile to the United States and the Vatican—remained aggressive? A vast, imperialistic empire of 290 million people armed with enough strategic and tactical nuclear weapons to incinerate our ashes a hundred times and then roll over them with miles of tanks and armored vehicles wasn't going to just disappear overnight. If anything, Communism seemed as firmly entrenched as ever.

About the time of the pope's visit, Soviet troops rolled into neighboring Afghanistan in tanks to prop up a puppet regime, and all President Jimmy Carter did in response was to withhold pole vaulters and other athletes from the Moscow Olympics.

A little later, when a Polish electrician named Lech Walesa led a strike in a shipyard at Gdansk, the new Polish leader, Gen. Wojciech Jaruzelski, hurried off to the Kremlin, where his Soviet taskmasters warned that if he didn't crush *Solidarity* with his men, they would with theirs. No doubt the Hungarian (1956) and the Czechoslovakian (1968) revolts helped remind the Polish general that his Soviet comrades had a history of invading their noncooperative European allies. Jaruzelski returned home, Walesa was arrested, *Solidarity* was crushed, and the general's mentors in Moscow were appeased.

Meanwhile, Saigon had become Ho Chi Minh City, and the Khmer Rouge took over Cambodia. Hailie Selassie's government in Ethiopia was replaced by Marxists, and the socialist Sandinistas gained power in Nicaragua. South Yemen had a Marxist government, and Fidel Castro—thumbing his nose at the *yanquis* in the north—sent Cuban troops to prop up a Marxist government in Angola.

In short, for most of the eighties, the Adventist scenario of the United States enforcing the mark of the beast on the world seemed at best far off—at worst, far out.

But then history detoured. Whether it was, as Mr. Fukuyama expressed it, "the end of history," could be debated, but that it was the end of history as everyone expected history to turn out was beyond debate. Conventional wisdom had it that the East and the West would eventually become embroiled in a conflict that would unleash nuclear weapons, and we'd annihilate each other. Not an unlikely scenario, all things considered. Yet one thing wasn't considered: that according to Scripture, an East-West nuclear holocaust was not how it was all going to end. Something, sooner or later, had to change—and, sooner or later, it did.

It began with a death. Leonid Brezhnev—the General Secretary of the Communist Party of the Soviet Union, the man credited with taking the Soviet Union from a position of military inferiority to military parity (maybe even superiority) with the United States—died. He was replaced by Yuri Andropov, who, despite rumors that he was a closet liberal, was a dark, hidden figure (most people in the West didn't even know he was married until they saw photos of his wife crying over his tomb). He was replaced by Konstantin Chernenko, a semi-catatonic octogenarian who looked embalmed when he took the job and, a few months later, he was.

Then a new face appeared, an obscure (to the West) minister of agriculture young enough not to need a cue card to say anything more complicated than "hello" and "goodbye." The face, birthmark included, belonged to Mikhail Gorbachev, and just as the Lord used Cyrus, "one of the truly enlightened rulers of ancient times,"[3] to fulfill His prophetic plans in that era, so He used Gorbachev to fulfill His plans in ours.

Of course, Gorby was no James Madison or Thomas Jefferson. He was a pragmatist who inherited an economic system that was fast turning the Soviet Union into the world's biggest banana republic—except they barely had bananas!

In 1976, traveling across the Soviet Union to Japan, I spent one evening in Chabarosk, population about 500,000, just below eastern Siberia. Early in the afternoon, I wandered through the streets looking for food. There were no restaurants, grocery stores, Pizza Huts, or Western (or even Eastern) Sizzlers. Not even a Hojos. In any American town of 50,000, much less 500,000, my problem would have been *choosing* a restaurant, not *finding* one. Eventually I wandered into a bakery and grabbed a stale heel off a splintery wooden shelf. The woman at the register used an abacus (an abacus!) to count change, and she didn't even have a bag to put the bread in. I pulled crumbs out of my pocket all the way to Yokohama.

Gorbachev, obviously, needed to make big changes. He did, and soon new words like *perestroika* and *glasnost* entered our vernacular (already they seem so outdated, which shows how fast things have changed). The old world order was unraveling faster than anyone, even Gorbachev, expected.

One incident a few years ago started to put things together. Though events as profound and far-reaching as what we saw in the Soviet Union and Eastern Europe had to have prophetic significance, I didn't know how. But on the morning of December 2, 1989, I picked up the *Washington Post* and saw the front-page headline: "Gorbachev, Pope Meet, Agree on Diplomatic Relations."[4]

Here was the president of the Soviet Union, now in the Vatican, meeting with the head of the Roman Catholic Church, whom he called "the moral leader of the world"? And here was the pope calling the meeting "a sign of the times that have slowly matured, a sign rich in promise"? It was a sign of the times all right . . .

In the Jesuit weekly, *America*, Francis X. Murphy wrote: "Should Pope Pius XII and Soviet dictator Joseph Stalin be looking down on current world affairs from a vantage point beyond the stars [notice he has Pius XII and Stalin in the same place!] they would be more than amazed to witness the current Soviet President greet the Roman Pontiff as 'Your Holiness,' and assert that the Pope was the most important religious leader in the world. . . . Their handshake in the papal library in the Vatican on Friday, December 1, 1989, orchestrated on television cameras for immediate global diffusion, will certainly go down in history as an instant that marked a decisive turnabout in human affairs."[5]

And though the furious pace of events has rendered the fruits of even that extraordinary encounter null and void, the meeting, up to that time, symbolized the prophetic trends. I immediately wrote in the *Adventist Review* that "if the current trends continue, especially at the present pace, we will witness a radical restructuring of the world order in a direction that seems to be setting the stage for final events in Bible prophecy."[6]

As it was, the trends *did* continue, but not at "the present pace." They moved faster and faster until this vast, imperialistic empire of 290 million people and tanks and vehicles *did* disappear, and almost overnight.

Once the empire collapsed, the relationship between America and the former Soviet Union changed, the relationship between

Europe and the former Soviet Union changed, and the relationship between America and Europe changed. Everything, militarily, politically, diplomatically, changed—and we entered into that gray, nebulous zone called "the new world order."

The phrase was popularized by President George Bush after Saddam Hussein turned Kuwait into Iraq's nineteenth province. On October 30, 1990, the president declared that the U.N. can "help bring about a new day . . . a new world order." In Prague that November, he said that the Gulf crisis offered a historic opportunity to forge "for all nations a new world order." In his State of the Union address, he mentioned the "long-held promise of a new world order." And speaking in Georgia to families of troops in the Gulf, the president asserted that "there is no place for lawless aggression in the Persian Gulf and in this new world order that we seek to create."

The expression itself had been around long before the president turned it into the verbal logo of the nineties (yours truly wrote about "a radical restructuring of the world order" [i.e., a new world order] in that *Review* article months before the president made the phrase famous). Everyone from David Rockefeller to Adolf Hitler has used the phrase or a reasonable facsimile thereof. On the back side of every dollar bill, below the Masonic symbols of the pyramid and the all-seeing eye, is the Latin *Novus Ordo Seclorum*, which can be translated, "new world order."

Actually, new world orders are not new. They have been cropping up all the time. The rise and fall of each major world empire, from the Persian Empire to the British and each one in between, ushered in a new world order, so why not the collapse of the Soviet as well? The world has not been static or stable since Ibbi-Sin's city of Ur was ravaged by the Elamites 500 years before Moses led the children of Israel out of Egypt. The political structure of the world has never been constant. Even today, half the countries of the world are less than forty years old.

"To peruse a nineteenth-century map of Europe," said an article in the *Atlantic*, "is to recognize the reckless impermanence of history, with its squandered Prussias, Bohemias, and city-statelets, its departed Hapsburg, czarist, and Ottoman realms. It would be unreasonable to think that a map drawn in the twenty-first century won't hold larger surprises."[7]

Though it has such a firm, authoritative sound, *the new world order* is about as objective as a Rorschach test. "Whatever cropped up post–cold war," wrote Fred Barnes in *The New Republic*, "that was the new world order."[8] For George Bush, the new world order entailed some fuzzy notion of collective security under the umbrella of the United Nations. Before he *glasnost*ed himself out of a job, Mikhail Gorbachev envisioned the new world order as a place where a Soviet union, renewed by democracy and *perestroika*, would play a positive and prosperous role within the brotherhood of nations. Even Pope John Paul II has his own notions of the new world order (see chapter 4).

When Bush first used the term, he probably thought of it as just a cute little expression like "points of light" or "read my lips." Though his administration stopped using it in 1991, the phrase has taken on a life of its own, especially among the left- and right-wing fringe who have done more speculating about these four syllables than they have over Henry Kissinger (the beast?) or Gorbachev's head blotch (the mark of the beast?).

Eustace Mullins, a far-right conspiracy theorist, warns that Bush's new world order idea is part of a scheme concocted by the one-worldism "Black Nobility," which consists of the British royal family, the Rothschilds, and the Rockefellers.

The Marxist *Revolutionary Worker* sees that phrase as the ominous code word for the capitalistic, running-dog, bourgeois Western imperialism that will take advantage of the post-Soviet world and exploit proletarians everywhere. One headline read: "The New World Order and the Pan Am 103 Scam," in which the paper warned that the United States framed Libya in the bombing as a pretext to bomb them.

The editor of the *Southern National Newsletter*, a Tennessee publication advocating a restoration of the confederacy, warns that the new world order is nothing but another "Yankee land grab."

Even preacher and Christian businessman Pat Robertson published a 268-page tome called, appropriately enough, *The*

New World Order. "I am equally convinced," he wrote, "that for the past two hundred years the term *new world order* has been the code phrase of those who desired to destroy the Christian faith and what Pope Pius XI termed 'the Christian social order.' They wish to replace it with an occult-inspired world socialist dictatorship."[9]

Whatever the new world order was supposed to be, the phrase did strike a chord among Adventists. It should, because ultimately, for prophecy to be fulfilled the way we have predicted, some type of new world order will have to be established.

> As the Sabbath has become the special point of controversy throughout Christendom, and religious and secular authorities have combined to enforce the observance of the Sunday, the persistent refusal of a small minority to yield to the popular demand will make them objects of universal execration. It will be urged that the few who stand in opposition to an institution of the church and a law of the state ought not to be tolerated; that it is better for them to suffer than for whole nations to be thrown into confusion and lawlessness. . . .
>
> This argument will appear conclusive; and a decree will finally be issued against those who hallow the Sabbath of the fourth commandment, denouncing them as deserving of the severest punishment and giving the people liberty, after a certain time, to put them to death.[10]

> As America, the land of religious liberty, shall unite with the papacy in forcing the conscience and compelling men to honor the false sabbath, the people of every country on the globe will be led to follow her example.[11]

Obviously, things will have to be different for these predictions to be fulfilled. The biblical warning that "he causeth all, both small and great, rich and poor, free and bond, to receive a mark in their right hand, or in their foreheads" (Revelation 13:16) could not have happened, according to our understanding, just a few years ago. Ellen White's warning, however, that "the final events will be rapid ones,"[12] should take on a whole new meaning, because recent events have proven that radical changes can happen faster than any of us imagined. It's no coincidence, either, that the collapse of the Soviet Empire fits squarely into our prophetic scenario. We should have known it was coming.

"If last year," I wrote in that *Review* article, "someone would have told me that within a year there would be a Solidarity government in Poland, that the Berlin Wall would be null and void, that the Communists would be losing power in Czechoslovakia, Hungary, East Germany, and Bulgaria, and that the Soviets would be encouraging these reforms—I would have thought I had backslidden, left the church, and was smoking pot!"[13]

If they had further told me that Communism would, two years later, be finished, not only in Eastern Europe but in the Kremlin itself; that the Soviet Union would no longer be soviet, must less a union; that all the republics would break away into independent nations; and that the Soviet Communist central government would disappear—I would have been sure I had backslidden, left the church, and was on LSD, not pot!

In 1980, during the old world order, I faced moments of raw doubt about the prophetic message. The Soviet Union was like a big brown bear crawling across the pages of Revelation and devouring our interpretation of chapters 13 and 14. During those moments, however, the Lord pointed me to the book of Daniel, chapters 2 and 7 in particular. Instantly, images of iron and clay toes, winged leopards, and talking horns spread out across my mind like a home video. The message was clear: the Lord *did indeed* rule over nations. If God was in such control that He could predict the rise and fall of the pagan Roman Empire centuries before the events, He could deal with the Soviet one as well.

So, reaching out in faith, grasping "the substance of things hoped for, the evidence of things not seen" (Hebrews 11:1), I uttered a prayer and pressed ahead, having unanswered questions but also a firm trust in God. Ten years later, as unexpected earth-shaking events unfolded before my eyes, most of those questions were answered, and that trust richly rewarded.

1. See Clifford Goldstein, *Best Seller* (Boise, Idaho: Pacific Press, 1990).

2. Clifford Goldstein, *The Saving of America* (Boise, Idaho: Pacific Press, 1988), 7, 8.

3. John Bright, *A History of Israel* (Philadelphia: Westminster, 1981), 362.

4. The *Washington Post*, 2 Dec. 1989, 1A.

5. Francis X. Murphy, C.SS.R.,"Aggiornamento to Perestroika: Vatican Ostpolitik," *America*, 19 May 1990, 494.

6. Clifford Goldstein, "Catholics, Communists, and Adventists," *Adventist Review*, 18 Jan. 1990, 5.

7. David Lawday, "My Country: Right . . . or What?" *Atlantic Monthly*, July 1991, 22.

8. Fred Barnes, "Brave New Gimmick," *The New Republic*, 25 Feb. 1991, 15.

9. Pat Robertson, *The New World Order* (Dallas: Word, 1991).

10. *The Great Controversy*, 615, 616.

11. Ellen G. White, *Testimonies to the Church* (Mountain View, Calif.: Pacific Press, 1948), 6:18.

12. Ibid., 9:11.

13. Goldstein, "Catholics, Communists, and Adventists," 5.

THREE:

The
New Rome

When the smoke, sand, and dust of Operation Desert Storm settled, the United States came out, not only on top of Iraq, but of the world. When just a few years ago pundits were bemoaning America's decline, they now refer to the United States as the world's premier military and political heavyweight. "The world's sole remaining superpower," said *Time* magazine,[1] an idea expressed by commentators everywhere. And not only is America *the* superpower, but, according to columnist Charles Krauthammer, there is "no prospect in the immediate future of any power to rival the United States."[2]

Talking about America's new role as the world's only superpower, Palestine Liberation Organization chief Yassir Arafat called Washington, D.C., "the new Rome."[3]

The new Rome! Why? Because the old Rome had been the unrivaled superpower of its age, and the United States is now in that position.

Arafat's words, of course, invoke the Adventist interpretation of prophecy. In Daniel 7, the prophet dreamed of four winds that "strove upon the great sea" (Daniel 7:2), out of which came four beasts. The first was "like a lion, and had eagles' wings"; the second was "like unto a bear" (verse 4); the third was "like a leopard" (verse 6); and the fourth was "dreadful and terrible, and strong exceedingly" and it had "ten horns" (verse 7). Out of that fourth beast arose a powerful little horn with "eyes like the eyes of man and a mouth speaking great things" (verse 8). This little horn "made war with the saints and prevailed against them" (verse 21). It "spoke great words against the most high," and the saints were delivered into its hand for "a time and times and half a time" (verse 25).

Daniel placed more emphasis on this little horn, and he gave more details concerning it, than for any other beast in this prophecy—a significant point, considering that the others symbolized great world empires: Babylon (lion), Medo-Persia (bear), Greece (leopard), fourth beast (pagan Rome). Why would the prophecy have accorded so much space to the little horn unless it was to be a major world player that would be equal to, or even exceed, the empires that preceded it?

The little horn, of course, was papal Rome. No other interpretation works. Those identifying the little horn as Seleucid king Antiochus IV Epiphanes might as well try making it fit Bugs Bunny. It's Rome!

In Revelation 13, imagery from Daniel 7 is repeated, linking the two chapters. "And I stood upon the sand of the *sea*, and saw a *beast rise up* out of the sea, having seven heads and *ten horns*" (Revelation 13:1). Already, three images from Daniel 7 reappear here: sea, rising beasts, ten horns.

"And the beast which I saw was like unto a *leopard*, and his feet were as the feet of a *bear*, and his mouth as the mouth of a *lion*" (verse 2). Again, we have images from Daniel 7—leopard, lion, and bear.

This beast in Revelation has a mouth "*speaking great things and blasphemies*; and power was given unto him to continue *forty and two months*" (verse 5). This beast also made "*war with the saints*," and overcame them (verse 7). The mouth speaking great things and blasphemies, the making war with the saints and overcoming them—all are images from Daniel 7. Even the "forty and two months" is another way of saying the "time, times and half a time" of Daniel 7.[4]

The composite beast in Revelation 13 is obviously the same power emphasized in Daniel 7—papal Rome.

However, in Revelation 13, another power immediately follows Rome: "And I beheld another beast coming up out of the earth, and he had two horns like a lamb, and he spake as a dragon" (verse 11). Though this nation starts out with gentle, lamblike qualities, it "speaks like a dragon." Adventists have always identified it as the United States, which will become an oppressive, persecuting power that *"exerciseth all the power of the first beast before him."* Who is that "first beast before him"? Rome. And America is now—*"the new Rome"*?

What makes this sudden ascension of America so exciting is that just a few years ago alarmists were decrying America's decline. *"Johnny can't read, Johnny can't write, Johnny can't fight"* was the warning. Japanese and German kids were smarter, better educated, better trained than their American counterparts, and thus the nation was declining.

Author Paul Kennedy, capturing the sentiment of economists, historians, and political scientists, warned that "Rome fell, Babylon fell, Scarsdale's turn will come."[5]

Fearful of America's decline, especially in the economic sphere, Paul Mead in 1990 wrote in *Harper's*: "I envision a world made up of three rival blocks: one based in the Western European nations; one dominated by Japan; and the American block, the weakest and most troubled."[6]

In 1987, James Chase wrote in the *Atlantic Monthly* that America was unwilling to "change the structure of alliances in a way that would honestly reflect a mature America's diminished role in the world."[7]

Expressed in a more common vernacular, John McLaughlin asked years ago, "Is America Going to the Dogs?"[8]

Now, of course, in the aftermath of the Gulf War, the myth of America's decline has been exposed. The United States has been losing its economic edge, no doubt, though Japan itself has been in a spiraling recession, and Germany has been hurt by the huge cost of reunification. Yet that still didn't stop America from leading the coalition against Saddam, when our rich rivals such as Japan and Germany were paralyzed by the conflict. Deutsche marks and Japanese yen, in and of themselves, didn't automatically translate into geopolitical power. Whatever its economic woes, America has assumed a leadership role, not only of the West, but almost the whole world.

"Before the Gulf crisis," Krauthammer wrote, "American

declinists were lamenting America's fall from its perch atop the world in—their favorite benchmark year—1950. Well, in 1950 the United States engaged in a war with North Korea. It lasted three years, cost 54,000 American lives, and ended in a draw. Forty-one years later the United States engaged in a war with Iraq, a country of comparable size. It lasted six weeks, cost 143 American lives, and ended in a rout. If the Roman Empire had declined at that rate, you'd be reading this in Latin."[9]

Of course, the Koreans (and the North Vietnamese) had the whole Communist world behind them; Iraq didn't. But that's the point. Had Saddam enjoyed the backing of the Soviets, the story would have ended differently. The U.S. wouldn't have risked World War III with Moscow just to put the emir of Kuwait back on his throne. With our major adversary gone, what other nation could stand up against the United States? None, which is why a National Public Radio correspondent called George Bush "the president of the world."

When a Marxist-led coalition overthrew a satellite regime in Ethiopia, whom did both sides call upon to mediate the takeover? The United States. When Boris Yeltsin took office, where was his first visit? The United States. When the Baltic states began their attempted breakaway, from whose constitution were they quoting? The constitution of the United States. When Bangladesh was devastated by storms and floods, whom did it seek for aid and succor? The United States. And when Saddam invaded Kuwait, whose military led the liberation? That of the United States.

These trends began even before the Gulf War, which didn't make America the new world leader; it simply revealed that, after the collapse of Soviet and Eastern European Communism, America already was.

Thus, writes Krauthammer, we now have "a highly unusual world structure with a single power, the United States, at the apex of the international system."[10] According to prophecy, the world will face a highly unusual situation when the United States forces the world to "worship the image of the beast."

The United States' unrivaled superpower status, "at the apex of the international system," fits perfectly into the Adventist scenario of the last days. By identifying the lamblike beast of Revelation 13:11 as the United States, our pioneers basically predicted that America would have to become the dominant political and military power. Otherwise, how could it enforce "the mark of the beast" upon the world?

The Adventist identification was remarkable for two reasons. First, it was made when other expositors envisioned America's role as a positive one. In *White Jacket* (1850), Herman Melville wrote, "We Americans are the peculiar, chosen people—the Israel of our time; we bear the ark of liberties of the world. . . . God has predestined, mankind expects, great things from our race; and great things we feel in our soul."[11] Joshua Strong proclaimed (1886) that in the United States "God is training the Anglo-Saxon race for its mission."[12]

Second, Adventists initially made their interpretation when the United States was hardly a world power, much less the dominant one.

In 1851, J. N. Andrews was the first Adventist in print to identify Protestant America as the power represented by the second beast. In "Thoughts on Revelation 13 and 14,"[13] Andrews identifies the two-horned beast of Revelation 13:11 as "our own country," the United States.

In 1884, Ellen White wrote that "the image of the beast represents another religious body clothed with similar power. The formation of this image is the work of that beast whose peaceful rise and mild professions render it so striking a symbol of the United States."[14]

In 1888, in *The Great Controversy*, she was even more forceful:

What nation of the New World was in 1798 rising into power, giving promise of strength and greatness, and attracting the attention of the world? The application of the symbol admits of no question. One nation, and only one, meets the specifications of this prophecy; it points unmistakably to the United States of America.[15]

If this interpretation, in which America would enforce the

mark of the beast upon the world, seemed implausible even ten years ago, how did it appear in the mid-1800s, when the big powers were still the old-world ones—Prussia, France, Austria-Hungary, and England? In 1851, when Andrews first published his identification of the two-horned beast, America had a peace-time army of about twenty thousand men, one-tenth the number of combatants at the Battle of Waterloo alone. In 1814 (less than forty years before his article), the British burned Washington, D.C. In 1867, Sitting Bull's braves wiped out General Custer's Seventh U.S. Cavalry Regiment. Thus, sixteen years *after* Andrews' prediction, and only eight years *before* Ellen White's (published in 1884), America was still fighting Indians, and not always so successfully, either. *And this was the nation that was going to force the world to make an image to the beast?*

Of course, the pioneers, Ellen White included, expected these events to happen in their lifetime, and indeed the Lord could have come back then. The point is merely that in the 1800s the fulfillment of these prophecies didn't *seem* as possible as it does today.

Not until World War I did the United States become an international force to be reckoned with. Nevertheless, even in 1933, when Hitler became führer, the United States had only the sixteenth largest army in the world—smaller than Spain's, Turkey's, even Poland's. After emerging victorious from World War II, America did enjoy unrivaled hegemony, but not for long, because the Soviet Union soon challenged it everywhere, including space. Older Americans remember *Sputnik* and the ensuing panic because the Reds were orbiting satellites over our heads while, as Tom Wolfe wrote in *The Right Stuff*, American "rockets always blew up."[16]

Once the Soviet Union became a superpower on a par with the United States, it was hard to see how America could ever fulfill its prophetic role. If, because of the Soviets, the U.S. couldn't kick Fidel out of Cuba, how could it ever enforce the mark of the beast upon the world?

Now, of course, the Soviet Union has disappeared, and with it the most implacable barrier to Adventist eschatology.

"America," wrote Jim Hoagland in the *Washington Post*, "would now determine all major global events."[17]

"I'd like us still to be," said President George Bush in 1992, "the undisputed leader of the world."[18] No doubt, President Bill Clinton would like it too.

In 1992, a classified Defense Plan Guidance document was leaked to the *New York Times* by "an official who believes this post-Cold-War strategy debate should be carried out in the public domain."[19] The forty-six-page document, later declassified, was an internal administration policy statement that planned America's military posture for the new world order. The gist of the document was that, now that the United States was the world's only superpower, it intended to stay that way.

"Our first objective," it said, "is to prevent the reemergence of a new rival, either on the territory of the former Soviet Union or elsewhere, that poses a threat of that posed formerly by the Soviet Union. This . . . requires that we endeavor to prevent any hostile power from dominating a region whose resources would, under consolidated control, be sufficient to generate global power."

The document said, too, that "the U.S. must show the leadership necessary to establish and protect a new order that holds the promise of convincing potential competitors that they need not aspire to a greater role or pursue a more aggressive posture to protect their legitimate interests. . . . Finally, we must maintain the mechanisms for deterring potential competitors from even aspiring to a larger regional global role."

Once public, the document faced a firestorm of criticism here and abroad. Especially piqued were Japan and Germany, two allies specifically mentioned as potential rivals who needed to be deterred from "aspiring to a larger regional or global role."

Because of the criticism, the document was revised. Released to the *Washington Post* in May 1992, the new version stressed the need for "like-minded nations" working together in a "collective response to preclude threats." Nevertheless, it stated that though allies were expected to take an appropriate share of responsibility in conflicts that directly affected them, the United States "must maintain the capabilities for addressing selectively those security problems that threaten our own interests." Though the specific references to deterring any potential rivals were deleted in the revised document, according to the *Washington Post*, "A senior official interviewed Friday said military readers will continue to perceive the 'clear messages' of the passages on Japan and Russia but 'without raising some of the froth' of the earlier draft."[20] The *Post* said, too, that many deletions were still held but not written down because, as one official put it, "this document apparently is uncapable of being kept among ourselves."

The Pentagon's logic, no matter how unpopular, makes sense. After World War II, Japan and Germany were crushed. The Soviet Union, though victorious, lost twenty million people and was no match for the United States. The U.S. alone possessed nuclear weapons, and it alone emerged from the war in good shape economically and militarily. Then for whatever reason, our leaders allowed the Soviet Union to become a military superpower on a par with the United States. The result was a forty-year standoff that cost America trillions of dollars, tens of thousands of lives, one stalemated war (Korea), one lost one (Vietnam), and a close brush with nuclear annihilation (the Cuban missile crisis).

With the lessons of the past so fresh in their minds, America's leaders would be foolish to allow anything like that to happen again. More than likely—they won't.

"If the new world order means anything," wrote Krauthammer, "it is an assertion of American interests and values in the world."[21]

America, of course, has values worth asserting—lamblike qualities such as democracy and religious freedom. Unfortunately, according to prophecy, this nation will speak like a dragon (see Revelation 13:11), and it will make "the earth and them which dwell therein to worship the first beast, whose deadly wound was healed" (verse 12).

With no rivals, and with the Cold War revealing why the U.S.

should allow none, America is better positioned now than ever to fulfill its role of causing "as many as would not worship the image of the beast" to be killed (Revelation 13:15).

It's not called "the new Rome" for nothing.

---

1. *Time*, 29 July 1991, 13.

2. Charles Krauthammer, "The Lonely Superpower," *The New Republic*, 29 July 1991, 23.

3. *Newsweek*, 12 Aug. 1991, 33.

4. See also Revelation 12:6 and 14. For a more detailed study of this prophecy, see *God Cares* (Pacific Press); *Selected Studies on Prophetic Interpretation* (Biblical Research Institute); *1844 Made Simple* (Pacific Press); and *The Prophetic Faith of Our Fathers* (Review and Herald).

5. Paul Kennedy, "The (Relative) Decline of America," *Atlantic Monthly*, August 1987, 33.

6. Paul Mead, "On the Road to Ruin," *Harper's*, March 1990, 61.

7. James Chase, "Ike Was Right," *Atlantic Monthly*, August 1987, 40.

8. John McLaughlin, "Is America Going to the Dogs?" *National Review*, 31 July 1987, 22.

9. Krauthammer, 24.

10. Ibid., 23.

11. Quoted in Paul Boyer, *When Time Shall Be No More* (Cambridge: Harvard University Press, 1992), 228.

12. Quoted in ibid., 229.

13. J. N. Andrews, "Thoughts on Revelation 13 and 14," *Second Advent Review and Sabbath Herald*, 19 May 1851.

14. Ellen G. White, *The Spirit of Prophecy* (Oakland: Pacific Press, 1884), 4:278.

15. *The Great Controversy*, 440.

16. Tom Wolfe, *The Right Stuff* (New York: Bantam, 1984), 201.

17. *Washington Post*, 29 Aug. 1991.

18. Quoted in *Atlantic Monthly*, August 1992, 22.

19. *Baltimore Sun*, 8 Mar. 1992, 13A.

20. *Washington Post*, 24 May 1992, A23.

21. Krauthammer, 26.

FOUR:

The Keys
of This Blood

For most of the twentieth century, the papacy remained in a sorry position to fulfill its prophetic role. Caught between the overwhelming idealogies of the Marxist East and the capitalist West, the Vatican hovered on the sidelines, a minor player amid the hardball geopolitics of the superpowers. It meddled where and when it could, and exerted influence hither and yon, but in a world where SAC bombers, cruise missiles, and MIGs ruled the heavens, the Vatican could do only so much on earth. Joseph Stalin best expressed the relative impotency of the papacy when he mocked, "How many divisions does the pope have?"

None, which was why until recently it was hard to imagine how the Vatican could ever fulfill its end-time role. Not until 1929, for example, did the papacy even regain sovereignty over the little 108.7 acres of Vatican City, and then only after Pius XI signed the Lateran Treaty, recognizing the fascist government of Benito Mussolini. That hardly sounds like the great power depicted in Revelation and *The Great Controversy*!

After World War II, the world divided into two hostile camps, one overtly hostile to Roman Catholicism. The pope could do nothing as half of Europe was swallowed by militant, atheistic Communism. How much power did the papacy wield when, in former staunchly Catholic countries, its members were persecuted, its churches closed, and its priests jailed, even killed? The pope, who claimed to be the vicar of Christ on earth, wasn't allowed to visit even much of his native continent.

Across the Atlantic, *Protestant* America, for years fiercely anti-Catholic, was becoming a gigantic political, economic, and military power. Anti-Catholicism had been so rooted in the American psyche that it was even reflected in the Declaration of Independence.[1] As late as 1966, when Pope Paul VI spoke at the United Nations, President Lyndon Johnson visited the pontiff at his hotel. Had St. Peter's successor come to the White House, there would have been an unholy uproar. Again, this hardly sounds like the world power depicted in Revelation.

Meanwhile, the United States and the Soviet Union, each amassing nuclear and conventional arsenals, faced off in the Cold War while Rome sat helplessly crunched between them.

But then European and Soviet Communism went belly up, and Pope John Paul II, more than any other man, was credited with turning them on their backs. "The Pope, not Gorbachev, Sparked Changes in Europe," read a headline in the *Jerusalem Post*.[2] *Time* magazine reported that "the Pope from Poland, John Paul II, did more than most to drive communism to its grave."[3] In the *Baltimore Sun*, William Pfaff wrote that "Freeing the East-block countries was from the start a principal theme of the papacy of Karol Wojtyla, after he was elected Pope John Paul II in 1978. His trips to Poland and elsewhere in the communist countries, and the response they evoked, were major factors in weakening the communist governments' claims to legitimacy."[4] Even Gorbachev admitted: "All that has happened in Eastern Europe over these last few years would not have been possible without the presence of this Pope."[5]

With so much credit to the pope for the monumental events that have created the post–Cold War new world order, no wonder the papacy now occupies a powerful position in it. And nowhere is the sudden rise of the papacy more graphically explained than in Malachi Martin's 1990 hardcover *The Keys of This Blood*.

From the earliest pages, Malachi Martin states that John Paul was hurling the papacy into the arena of international politics as it hadn't experienced since the Dark Ages.

"It was," Martin wrote, "the first distinguishing mark of

John Paul's career as Pontiff that he had thrown off the straight-jacket of papal inactivity in world affairs."[6] He said, too, that John Paul "had served notice that he intended to take up and effectively exercise once more the international role that had been central to the tradition of Rome, and to the very mandate Catholics maintain was conferred by Christ upon Peter and upon each of his successors."[7]

Early in John Paul's pontificate, commentators saw the trend. In 1980 the *Atlantic* said that John Paul "has without a doubt returned the Vatican to the center of the international stage."[8] In 1979, Catholic columnist George Will wrote that "in the last quarter of this secularizing century, the world's most galvaniz-ing man works at an altar. Today power is associated with prosaic men governing great states, all of whom must envy the power of the poet whose 'state' is a Rome neighborhood."[9]

According to Martin, the pope sees himself, not as one world leader among many, but as the one who, by virtue of his posi-tion, should be the preeminent world religious and political authority. "That authority," wrote Martin, "that strength, is symbolized in the Keys of Peter, washed in the blood of the God-man Jesus Christ. John Paul is and will be the sole possessor of the Keys of this Blood on that Day."[10]

What day? The day when John Paul assumes the political supremacy that he believes his office entitles him to. "For in the final analysis," wrote Martin, "John Paul II as the claimant Vicar of Christ does claim to be the ultimate court of judgment on the society of states as a society."[11]

According to Martin, the essence of John Paul's new world order is that neither oppressive Marxism with its godless idealogy, nor materialistic capitalism with its financial inequi-ties, are acceptable, and both must go. "The primary difficulty for Pope John Paul in both these models for the new world order," wrote Martin, "is that neither of them is rooted in the moral laws of human behavior revealed by God through the teaching of Christ, as proposed by Christ's Church [i.e., the Roman Catholic Church]."[12]

In his first social encyclical (*Centesimus Annus*) since the collapse of Eastern European Communism, the pope stated the problems with both systems: "The historical experience of the West shows that even if the Marxist analysis and its foundations of alienation are false, nevertheless alienation—and the loss of the authentic meaning of life—is a reality in western societies too. This happens in consumerism, when people are ensnared in a web of false and superficial gratification rather than being helped to experience their personhood in an authentic and concrete way."[13]

He also stressed the need for Sunday laws. "[O]ne may ask whether existing laws and the practice of industrialized societies effectively ensure in our own day the exercise of this basic right to Sunday rest."[14]

Writing encyclicals, of course, doesn't make you a world power. Now, though, with the end of European and Soviet Communism, with the present instability in international finance, with the moral decline of the West, the world—linked by massive communication facilities—is heading in a direction that could grant such an internationally revered figure as John Paul (or a successor) the unparalleled political authority he's expending all the powers of his pontificate to get. Ultimately, according to Revelation 13:1-3, something to that effect must happen. The composite beast of Revelation 13, the papacy, received a wound: "And I saw one of his heads as it were wounded to death" (Revelation 13:3). That wound, however, is not permanent: "And his deadly wound was healed: and all the world wondered after the beast" (verse 3).

For "fifteen hundred years and more," Martin wrote, "Rome had kept as strong a hand as possible in each local community around the wide world. . . . By and large, and admitting some exceptions, that had been the Roman view until two hundred years of inactivity had been imposed upon the papacy by the major secular powers of the world."[15]

Two hundred years of inactivity imposed upon the papacy by the major secular powers of the world?

Two hundred years ago was the 1790s. Adventists have dated the deadly wound given to Rome (see Revelation 13:3)—at the end of the "time, times and dividing of time" of Daniel 7:25 (see also Revelation 12:6 and 13:5)—in 1798, when French general Berthier took the pope captive. Or, about two hundred years ago!

Ellen White, in *The Great Controversy*, warned that the "Roman Church is far-reaching in her plans and modes of operation. She is employing every device to extend her influence and increase her power in preparation for a fierce and determined conflict to regain control of the world."[16] This pope, says Martin, is in a struggle over who "will hold and wield the dual power of authority and control over each of us as individuals and over all of us together as a community; over the entire six billion people expected by demographers to inhabit the earth by early in the third millennium."[17]

Her words that "it is a part of her [Rome's] policy to assume the character that will best accomplish her purposes"[18] take on an interesting dimension in contrast to this statement by Martin: "John Paul had a certain invaluable immunity from the suspicious and prying eye. That white robe and skullcap, the Fisherman's ring on his index finger, the panoply of papal liturgy, the appanage of pontifical life, all mean that rank and file of world leaders, as well as most observers and commentators, would see him almost exclusively as a religious leader."[19]

"She [the papacy] has clothed herself in Christlike garments,"[20] Ellen White warned; said Martin: "John Paul's rockbound certitude—deriving from his Catholic faith and from his personal endowment as the sole Vicar of God among men—is that any human effort that is not ultimately based on the moral and religious teaching of Christ must fail."[21]

"Rome is aiming to re-establish her power," said Ellen White, "to recover her lost supremacy. . . . She is silently growing into power. Her doctrines are exerting their influence in legislative halls, in the churches, and in the hearts of men. . . . Stealthily and unsuspectedly she is strengthening her forces to further her own ends."[22] Martin writes that John Paul planned "to endow his papacy with an international profile and, as Pope, move around among world leaders and nations, vindicating a position for himself as a special leader among leaders, because in that competition he plans to emerge the victor."[23]

"The Roman church has not relinquished her claim to supremacy,"[24] said Ellen White. Wrote Martin: "John Paul II as the claimant Vicar of Christ does claim to be the ultimate court of judgment on the society of states as a society."[25]

"Marvelous in her shrewdness and cunning is the Roman Church. She can read what is to be. She bides her time,"[26] said Ellen White. Wrote Martin: "He is a pope who is waiting. That is the essence of his action."[27]

"A large class," Ellen White said, "even of those who look upon Romanism with no favor, apprehend little danger from her power and influence."[28] Wrote Martin: "No one, individual or corporate body, has formally conceded him the right to act and speak as a religious authority and moral monitor of the society of nations. He has assumed the mantle, and no one of consequence really disputes his assumption of it."[29]

What gives *The Keys of This Blood* extra punch is that the author is not some overenthusiastic-date-setting-imminent-Sunday-law-Seventh-day-Adventist trying to cram present-day events into our prophetic scenario. Malachi Martin is a devout Catholic (he dedicated his book to "The Immaculate Heart"), a former Jesuit who loves his church and is concerned about its future. His devout Catholicism, of course, gives the book a slant in favor of the pope and the Roman church, and the reader has to wonder about the accuracy of every detail in a 698-page book on current events that gives no references or footnotes.

Nevertheless, what's important is that the gist of *The Keys of This Blood*—written by someone probably not acquainted with the intricacies of the three angels' messages—is that Pope John Paul II is involved in an international struggle to gain the political supremacy that he believes his office entitles him to, and that, so far, as a figure of gargantuan proportions, he has been meeting with unparalleled success.

Others have noticed these trends too, even if they don't have our insights. Dave Hunt is a popular evangelical writer whose works include *The Seduction of Christianity* and a powerful exposé of Mormonism, *The God Makers*. He believes in the secret rapture, Armageddon as a geographical Middle Eastern

battle, and the centrality of the Jewish nation in Bible prophecy. In one of his latest books, however, Hunt comes to some
"Adventist" conclusions.

When most Christians have been looking at everyone from
Henry Kissinger to Gorbachev to some "Syrian Jew" as the
antichrist, Hunt wrote in *Global Peace and the Rise of the
Antichrist*: "And here is where the plot thickens. If the Antichrist will indeed pretend to be Christ, then his followers must
be Christians."[30] He becomes more candid: "In fact, by 'Christianity' both Gorbachev and the Pope mean *Roman Catholicism*
[italics his]. That just happens to be the official world religion of
the Roman Empire—the very religion that must recover that
status in preparation for the Antichrist. . . . The church and
'Christianity' of ancient Rome are being resurrected before our
very eyes with the blessing of the leaders of the world religions
and leading Protestants as well."[31]

Hunt sounds at times like *The Great Controversy*: "Thus
the power that Rome holds over its subjects is far greater
than that of any secular government over its citizens. When
the time comes to make a choice concerning where one's real
loyalty lies, there is little doubt of the outcome for the Catholic of whatever citizenship."[32] Wrote Ellen White in *The Great
Controversy*: "Whatever their nationality or their government, they [Roman Catholics] are to regard the authority of
the church as above all other. Though they may take the
oath pledging their loyalty to the state, yet back of this lies
the vow of obedience to Rome, absolving them of every pledge
inimical to her interests."[33]

According to Hunt, Rome hasn't changed her doctrines either: "The heretical doctrines of salvation that provoked the
Reformation were not changed and the cultic grip of the church
was actually tightened."[34] Ellen White wrote: "Romanism as a
system is no more in harmony with the gospel of Christ now
than at any former period in her history."[35]

Hunt also laments how Protestants are so accepting of the
Catholic religion: "The horrible deception is made all the
more persuasive and destructive by Protestant leaders sug-
gesting that the Roman Catholic Church preaches the bibli-

cal gospel. For example, the host of a popular Christian TV show (who heads the world's largest Christian television network) frequently gives viewers the false impression that Roman Catholic doctrine is no different from that of evangelicals. On one program, while interviewing three Catholic leaders, the host declared that the difference between Protestant and Catholic doctrines was merely 'a matter of semantics.'"[36] Ellen White said that "there is an increasing indifference concerning the doctrines that separate the reformed churches from the papal hierarchy; the opinion is gaining ground that, after all, we do not differ so widely on vital points as has been supposed."[37]

Hunt wrote, "The fact that Catholicism is taking over from Communism is hardly a cause for rejoicing; it is a strategic and necessary move. The Roman Empire cannot be revived without Catholicism *recovering* its dominant role" [italics supplied]."[38] Then, in language that makes *The Great Controversy* sound tame, he writes that "Communism had actually not been the worst enemy of Christianity. That distinction belongs to the 'whore of Babylon,' which claims to be 'Christian' yet has sent far more souls to hell than Marxism, with which it has much in common. Ironically, the Roman Catholic Church is as totalitarian as Communism ever was."[39]

Before the August 1991 coup in Moscow, Hunt wrote: "Whatever the future of Communism, the world is not destined to come under the dominion of a Marxist dictator, but of Antichrist. Atheism will not triumph, but a false religion. And the Roman Catholic Church will play a key role in bringing this about, and thus in determining mankind's destiny."[40]

In Poland, for instance, now that the Communists are out, the church is reestablishing dominion. *Time* magazine wrote that in Poland the church is "omnipresent and, in the view of some, virtually omnipotent." The article said, too, that the new power of Rome "has left many Poles uneasily wondering whether their country might someday be transformed into a clerical state, ruling in accordance with the dicta of Pope John Paul II."[41]

"The influence of Rome in the countries that once acknowledged her dominion," Ellen White wrote, "is still far from being destroyed."[42]

Already, in Eastern Europe, Adventists have tasted life under John Paul's new world order. When, in early 1992, Potomac Conference evangelist Tony Mavrakos held an evangelistic series in Kosice, Czechoslovakia, local Catholic priests told the people to avoid the meetings, which were held at the "White House," the Communist Party's former regional headquarters. When initial admonitions failed, the local bishop read an edict, naming Mavrakos himself, which warned that Catholics caught at the series would be excommunicated. They even ran newspaper advertisements against him. According to Mavrakos, the local conference president said that a letter came directly from the pope to the bishops, in which the Holy Father sternly admonished the people against attending.

Over a century ago, Ellen White in *The Great Controversy* precisely explained today's trends: "History testifies of her [the papacy's] artful and persistent efforts to insinuate herself into the affairs of nations."[43] Wrote Catholic historian Francis X. Murphy in 1990: "Convinced that the church must address *political* as well as religious issues, John Paul has made over forty-five overseas journeys and has maintained contact with as many governments and peoples as possible, insisting that the Holy See is inimical to no nation or people."[44]

"The Roman Church," Ellen White wrote, "now presents a fair front to the world, covering with apologies her record of horrible cruelties."[45] On the World Day of Peace, January 1, 1991, Pope John Paul delivered a message on religious liberty that sounded better than Thomas Jefferson: "It is essential," he said, "that the right to express one's own religious convictions publicly and in all domains of civil life be ensured if human beings are to live together in peace. . . . No human authority has the right to interfere with a person's conscience. . . . Truth imposes itself solely by the force of its own truth. . . ." Then, talking about persecution, he said, "As for religious intolerance, it cannot be denied that, despite the firm teaching of the Catholic Church according to which no one ought to be compelled to believe, throughout the centuries conflicts have occurred between Christians and members of other religions. This was formally acknowledged by the Second Vatican Council which stated that 'in the life of the People of God as it has made its way through the vicissitudes of human history, there have at times appeared ways of acting which were less in accord with the ways of the gospel.'"[46]

On his first visit to Czechoslovakia, the pope called for "a common European home from the Atlantic to the Urals," and also expressed confidence that Europe will "fully restore those human and Christian values which made its history glorious and enabled it to have a beneficial influence also on the other countries of the world."[47] At the end of 1991 he gathered, for the first time in history, all the Roman Catholic bishops of both Eastern and Western Europe in an attempt to fulfill his vision—"the re-Christianization of the Western countries."[48] During a four-day symposium in Rome, the pope said that a rediscovery of "Christian roots is the key to a united Europe."[49]

Of course, by "Christian values" he means Roman Catholic Christian values, and by "Christian roots" he means Roman Catholic roots, and by "re-Christianization" he means reestablishing Catholic dominion.

Recently, an Italian newspaper ran an article about KGB operations in Italy during the Cold War. Former KGB general Boris Solomatin, who oversaw the KGB's Italian work from 1976 to 1982, said that "the Vatican is a real superpower to be watched."[50]

"This world," John Paul told Czechoslovaks, "must be conquered."[51]

It will be, even if not everyone cooperates. Martin wrote in *The Keys of This Blood* that certain religions have "a deeply rooted opposition amounting to a nourished enmity for all that John Paul represents as a Churchman and a geopolitican." Among them, he wrote, are "Seventh-day Adventists."[52]

Martin makes an interesting statement about these opposition groups: "John Paul looks upon them with a special solicitude. But he knows that as they now stand, their future lies down one of two pathways. Either they will remain lodged in their *historical crevasses, holding on to their traditions.* Or, as some of them have shown a willingness to do, they will decide to accept some form of merger with the various tides advancing upon their positions. Beyond that, any satisfactory relief of their pathos must await near future historical events of a worldwide magnitude"[53] (italics supplied).

Martin doesn't mention what those events of worldwide magnitude will be, nor how those who insist on remaining lodged "in their historical crevasses" (seventh-day Sabbath?) will fare. He doesn't need to. We already know.

"As the Sabbath," Ellen White wrote in *The Great Controversy*, "has become the special point of controversy throughout Christendom, and religious and secular authorities have combined to enforce the observance of the Sunday, the persistent refusal of a small minority ["lodged in their historical crevasses"] to yield to the popular demand will make them objects of universal execration. It will be urged that the few who stand in opposition to an institution of the church and a law of the state ought not to be tolerated; that it is better for them to suffer than for whole nations to be thrown into confusion and lawlessness."[54]

"[I]t has always been an essential practice for Rome," wrote Martin, "to make decisions on the premise that the good of the geocommunity must take precedence *over all local advantages.* International politics might be driven and regulated according to the benefits to be derived by certain groups or nations at *the cost of others.*"[55]

What might that cost to others be?

"And he had power to give life unto the image of the beast, that the image of the beast should both speak, and cause that as many as would not worship the image of the beast should be killed" (Revelation 13:15).

Apparently, the pope (whichever one he is) will have all the divisions he needs.

---

1. See William Lee Miller, *The First Liberty* (New York: Alfred A. Knopf, 1986), 281, 282.

2. *Jerusalem Post*, 21 April 1990, 2.

3. *Time*, 13 May 1991.

4. *Baltimore Sun*, 20 Jan. 1992, 7A.

5. "Pope Was Vital to Fall of Communism, Says Gorbachev," Newsnet Item 18:391, 2 Mar. 1992, Reuters News Service.

6. Malachi Martin, *The Keys of This Blood* (New York: Simon and Schuster, 1990), 23.

7. Ibid., 22.

8. *Atlantic Monthly*, May 1980, 43.

9. *Newsweek*, 15 Oct. 1979, 4.

10. *Keys*, 639.

11. Ibid., 375.

12. Ibid., 19.

13. *Centesimus Annus* Origins: CNS Documentary Service, 16 May 1991, 16.

14. Ibid., 6.

15. *Keys*, 22.

16. *The Great Controversy*, 565, 566.

17. *Keys*, 15.

18. *The Great Controversy*, 571.

19. *Keys*, 23.

20. *The Great Controversy*, 571.

21. *Keys*, 345.

22. *The Great Controversy*, 581.

23. *Keys*, 480.

24. *The Great Controversy*, 448.

25. *Keys*, 375.

26. *The Great Controversy*, 580.

27. *Keys*, 639.

28. *The Great Controversy*, 572.

29. *Keys*, 492.

30. Dave Hunt, *Global Peace and the Rise of the AntiChrist* (Eugene, Ore.: Harvest House, 1990), 8.

31. Ibid., 105.

32. Ibid., 116.

33. *The Great Controversy*, 580.

34. Hunt, 139.

35. *The Great Controversy*, 565.

36. Hunt, 145.

37. *The Great Controversy*, 563.

38. Hunt, 135.

39. Ibid.

40. Ibid., 146.

41. *Time*, 20 May 1991, 40.

42. *The Great Controversy*, 579.

43. Ibid., 580.

44. Murphy, 496.

45. *The Great Controversy*, 571.

46. Message of His Holiness Pope John Paul II for the Celebration of the World Day of Peace (January 1, 1991).

47. "John Paul Announces Historic Synod of All European Bishops," *Religious News Service*, 23 April 1990, 4.

48. *Baltimore Sun*, 20 Jan. 1992, 7A.

49. "Pope: Christians' Roots Are Key to United Europe," *Religious News Service*, 5 Nov. 1991, 8.

50. *National and International Religion Report*, 23 Mar. 1992.
51. *Washington Post*, 23 April 1990, A19.
52. *Keys*, 286.
53. Ibid., 288.
54. *The Great Controversy*, 615.
55. *Keys*, 22, emphasis supplied.

FIVE:

The
Holy Alliance

The subtitle of *The Keys of This Blood*, published in 1990, reads: "The Struggle For World Dominion Between Pope John Paul II, Mikhail Gorbachev & The Capitalist West." Since then, the competition has dwindled by a third as Gorbachev couldn't retain dominion over his own country, much less the world. According to Martin's scenario (which seems to be happening), only two contenders for world dominion remain: the capitalist West (led by the United States) and John Paul II (the leader of Roman Catholicism)—the two powers depicted in Revelation and *The Great Controversy* that eventually do control the world!

Though Martin has Rome and the United States competing for world dominion, *Time* magazine showed them cooperating, which, according to prophecy, is what will ultimately happen. The magazine, with a picture of Pope John Paul II and Ronald Reagan on the cover, ran the headline: "Holy Alliance: How Reagan and the Pope conspired to assist Poland's Solidarity movement and hasten the demise of Communism."

The gist of the article was that from 1982 until the collapse of Polish Communism, the United States and the Vatican, under the leadership Pope John Paul II and President Ronald Reagan, cooperated in a clandestine operation to free Poland from Communism and loosen the Soviet hold upon Eastern Europe.

"This was one of the great secret alliances of all time," said Richard Allen, Reagan's first national security adviser, who was part of the team that worked with the pope.[1]

The article, though dealing specifically with politics, indirectly introduced another aspect of prophecy: the union of Protestants and Catholics. Without the diminishing of hostilities, which has established an unprecedented atmosphere of friendship and cooperation between Catholics and Protestants, this "Holy Alliance" probably would have never happened. The *Time* issue symbolizes, then, not just the political alliance between the United States and the Vatican, but also the growing rapprochement between Protestants and Catholics.

"Romanism," Ellen White wrote in *The Great Controversy*, "is now regarded by Protestants with far greater favor than in former years."[2]

"Recent attitudes toward Roman Catholics," wrote *Christianity Today* senior editor Kenneth Kantzer, "have become cautiously tolerant."[3]

More than just tolerant. Despite differences in theology, Catholics and Protestants over the past decades have been uniting where they can, especially on social issues.

"If Catholicism is to become more Catholic in the future," wrote David Wells in *Eternity* magazine, "which is what I expect under the present pope, then theological differences will become sharper but our alliances with Catholics against the secular culture can become deeper. I, for one, am ready for the trade off."[4]

In the introduction to *Evangelical Catholics,* by Catholic layman Keith Fournier, Chuck Colson wrote, "It's high time that all of us who are Christians come together regardless of the differences of our confessions and our traditions and make common cause to bring Christian values to bear in our society. When the barbarians are scaling the walls, there is no time for *petty quarreling* in the camp."[5] Apparently, for Colson, all that separates Catholics and Protestants is "petty quarreling."

Pat Robertson, too, promotes unity with Catholics on issues of common concern. "I believe frankly," Robertson said, "that the evangelicals and the Catholics in America, if they work together, can see many pro-family initiatives in our society, and we can be an effective counterbalance to some of the radical, leftist initiatives."[6]

In that same *Christianity Today* editorial, Kantzer continued: "Finally we [Catholics and evangelicals] can work together on those political and social issues where we are in such strong agreement. . . . Our united effort in these areas will do much to influence the world to the good. . . . In spite of basic differences, we can use our common Judeo-Christian value system to forge moral leadership that will advance the cause of justice and peace through a stable society in our nation and around the world."[7]

William Bentley Ball, noted constitutional lawyer and lay Catholic, wrote an article in *Christianity Today* called, "Why Can't We Work Together?" in which he stressed that conservative Catholics and evangelicals hold many doctrines in common: the divinity of Christ, the virgin birth, the Holy Spirit, the inerrancy of the Bible, the existence of Satan, and man's salvation through Christ. He might as well have added Sunday sacredness and the immortality of the soul.

"From these common beliefs," he explained, "many Catholics and many evangelicals derive clear positions on issues of law and public policy."[8]

"The opinion is gaining ground," wrote Ellen White, "that, after all, we do not differ so widely upon vital points as has been supposed."[9]

"In recent years," said a Catholic periodical, "evangelicals and Catholic groups have joined forces at every level of social action—from grassroots protests to lobbying Congress for changes in public policy—and have prevailed on a variety of shared concerns."[10]

One example of the political alliance between Catholics and Protestants occurred in April 1992, when Roman Catholic and Southern Baptist leaders—representing the two largest religious groups in the United States, groups not historically amicable—filed an amicus (friend-of-the-court) brief, urging "a thorough constitutional reconsideration" of abortion law in the United States.[11]

Besides the shared political and social thrust, another means of reconciliation between Protestants and Catholics has arisen: the notion of Catholics as evangelicals.

"If, like myself, you count yourself a Protestant in the Reformed tradition," wrote Colson in Keith Fournier's book, "you may be surprised to find yourself more at home with Keith's thinking than with that of many of your Protestant brothers and sisters. If you are an orthodox Catholic, you may find that you are truly part of the evangelical camp."[12]

Though numerous factors are involved in this idea of "Evangelical Catholics," a predominating one has been the burgeoning charismatic movement among Roman Catholics. Over the past few decades, the influx of sixty million Catholics worldwide into the charismatic movement has done more to break down barriers than any factor since Vatican Council II. Who cares if they pray the rosary, confess sins to priests, and believe that the pope is infallible—if they speak in "tongues" and manifest other "gifts," then Jesus must be working in their lives. They have the "baptism of the Holy Spirit," and that's what counts.

"Protestant and Catholic charismatic teaching on the Christian life," wrote *Christianity Today* senior editor J. I. Packer, "is to all intents and purposes identical. Is this not significant for the Christian future?"[13]

It's not hard to see how the charismatic movement can form the bridge. Charismatics have always tended to emphasize spiritual gifts at the expense of doctrine. A typical charismatic church could be filled with premillennials, amillennials, postmillennials, mid-premillennials, mid-postmillennials, and on and on. Outside of a few basics, such as the divinity of Christ, the devil, the Holy Spirit (all of which Catholics believe), charismatics can disagree on just about every other doctrine. The important thing is to be "filled with the Spirit." That overrides doctrinal differences, even with Roman Catholics.

The Catholic charismatic movement doesn't seem to be a passing fad, either. In June of 1992, seventeen thousand Catholic charismatics gathered in Pittsburgh to celebrate the twenty-fifth anniversary of the movement.[14] Catholic charismatics have been accepted by the Vatican, with the full blessing of Pope John Paul II. The International Charismatic Renewal Office occupies space at the Vatican.

Charismatic conferences, held the world over, burgeon with Catholics, who claim that their charismatic gifts have "deepened their experience of the rosary and of the Mass, and increased their devotion to Mary."[15] Priests, nuns, even monks raise hands, speak in "tongues," and utter "prophecies." At a charismatic gathering in New Orleans in 1987, half the participants were Roman Catholics, as were many speakers. Charismatic leader Vison Synan called these conferences "the only major meeting of its kind in the world where Protestants and Catholics get together."[16]

"The time was when Protestants placed a high value upon the liberty of conscience which had been so dearly purchased," Ellen White wrote in *The Great Controversy*. "They taught their children to abhor popery and held that to seek harmony with Rome would be disloyalty to God. But how widely different are the sentiments now expressed!"[17]

"I have found," said Billy Graham, "many people in the Roman Catholic church, both clergy and laity, who I believe are born again Christians. They may hold different theological views than I hold, but I believe they are in the body of Christ. So I consider them my brothers and sisters in Christ."[18]

Even Ellen White wrote that "there are real Christians in the Roman Catholic communion,"[19] but she said that of these "many will yet take their position with His [God's] people"[20] after receiving the truth. That's not what Billy Graham meant.

Many Catholics regard themselves as true evangelicals. "Futhermore, my identity as a Catholic Christian," wrote Keith Fournier, "is necessarily evangelical. I am 'evangelical' because I am on fire to proclaim the good news of Jesus Christ. As I said earlier, the word *evangelical* must not be reserved for one small segment of Christians. Rather, it should be the proud adjective of all Christian people."[21] Apparently, more and more Protestants would agree.

Ellen White's warning in *The Great Controversy* that Catholics and Protestants, burying hostilities, would draw together has become a reality. She never said there would have to be complete doctrinal harmony; she said merely that they would unite on common points, which is what's happening. Eventually they will join in an effort to promote Sunday legislation. Meanwhile, they're uniting when and where they can. The headlines have been so common for years: "Anglicans call for unity under the Pope"[22]; "Lutherans Ask Pope for Shared Communion"[23]; "New Signals About Reunification"[24]; "Catholic and Lutheran Bishops Will Hold Joint Worship."[25]

What's astounding about these events in light of *The Great Controversy* is that basic Catholic doctrine has not changed. Rome has not renounced, or even diluted, the Mass, transubstantiation, auricular confession, devotion to Mary (if anything, that has skyrocketed), the immaculate conception, Mary's bodily assumption into heaven, purgatory, papal infallibility, papal primacy, and the Roman church as the final interpreter of Scripture.

"But Romanism," wrote Ellen White a century ago, ". . . is no more in harmony with the gospel of Christ now than at any former period."[26]

Numerous meetings on justification by faith, the doctrine that first split the church, have been held between Catholic and Protestant scholars, and formal declarations of harmony are occasionally read, but these are mostly debates about semantics (We Adventists argue the same issues among ourselves), with the Catholic position not changing. Rome today remains what she has been for centuries: a sacramental church, which means that for her, salvation comes only through her hierarchial-sacramental mediation. You have to do certain things to be justified, and do them only through the church. At Vatican II, when the Catholic Church "loosened up," the Council compared the Roman church to the Incarnate Redeemer. The church was instituted, it said, "as a universal sacrament of salvation."

And this is the church that many Protestants accept as evangelical?

"There has been a change," Ellen White wrote in *The Great Controversy*, "but the change is not in the papacy."[27]

John Paul, despite all his talk about the unity of the body of Christ, is a conservative dogmatist showing little inclination to compromise. Apparently he doesn't have to, for Protestants seem to be taking Rome just as it is. And, according to inspiration, that's how they are going to get it.

Just as it is.

---

1. *Time*, 24 Feb. 1992, 28.

2. *The Great Controversy*, 563.

3. Kenneth Kantzer, "Church on the Move," *Christianity Today*, 7 Nov. 1986, 16.

4. David Wells, "Catholicism at the Crossroads," *Eternity*, September 1987, 14.

5. Keith Fournier, *Evangelical Catholics* (Nashville: Thomas Nelson, 1990), vi, emphasis supplied.

6. Quoted in *Church and State*, Aug. 1988, 15.

7. Kantzer, 17.

8. William Bentley Ball, "Why Can't We Work Together?" *Christianity Today*, 16 July 1990, 23.

9. *The Great Controversy*, 563.

10. Glenn Ellen Duncan, *Catholic Twin Circle*, quoted in *Church and State*, March 1989, 17.

11. *Religious News Service*, 6 April 1992, 5.

12. Fournier, vi.

13. J. I. Packer, "Rome's Persistent Renewal," *Christianity Today*, 22 June 1992, 19.

14. Religious News Service, 12 June 1992, 7.

15. *Christianity Today*, 21 Nov. 1986, 26.

16. *Religious News Service*, 22 July 1987, 22.

17. *The Great Controversy*, 563.

18. *Time*, 28 May 1990, 13.

19. *The Great Controversy*, 565.

20. Ibid.

21. Fournier, 49.

22. Dallas *Times Herald*, 1 Oct. 1989.

23. *Religious News Service*, 29 Oct. 1992, 1.

24. *Time*, 17 Mar. 1986.

25. *Religious News Service*, 24 April 1992.

26. *The Great Controversy*, 565.

27. Ibid., 571.

SIX:

The New Christian Right: Born Again?

At first glance, it seemed too good to be true. Jerry Falwell, once the scourge of liberals, feminists, humanists, homosexuals, Bolsheviks, Democrats, and atheists, was busy watering down the evangelical postulates of Liberty University in order to finagle sixty million dollars in tax money for his financially floundering school.[1] New Christian Right organizations such as the National Christian Action Council, Moral Majority, and the Freedom Council, each founded to "save America," couldn't save themselves. All have gone belly up, along with such publications as the *Fundamentalist Journal* and *Conservative Digest*. Jimmy Bakker's weakness for money, and Jimmy Swaggart's for women, helped sink contributions to the New Right's political juggernaut faster than the American electorate sank Pat Robertson's 1988 presidential campaign. And, even after twelve years of Reagan and Bush, the New Right, once dubbed "the centerpiece of the conservative movement,"[2] appears to have backslidden into political oblivion.

Appearances, however, can be deceiving. Indeed, far from being defunct, the New Christian Right is more entrenched in the American political system now than ever before.

"[T]he Evangelical Right is back," wrote Thomas Atwood, editor of *Policy Review*, "better organized for state and local politics and less dependent upon highly visible national leaders, and more effective because it works through broader based organizations not explicitly identified with Evangelicalism."[3]

"In the 1980s," says political scientist Matthew Moen, "the

New Right altered the public dialogue and the congressional debate. In the nineties, it is quietly infiltrating the power structure in order to gain influence in ways that it wasn't able to previously. And in some respects, with this new strategy, it is stronger now than ever before."[4]

A new strategy was needed. Despite the overnight proliferation of an alphabet soup of New Right organizations (NICPAC, ACTV, NCAC, CLEAR-TV, CV, CWA, CSFC, FCPAC, CMA, NCAP, EF, AFC, NPFC), massive fund-raising campaigns, and intense lobbying in Washington, D.C., the New Right for the whole eighties decade and into the early nineties achieved none of its major legislation, except, perhaps, the defeat of the Equal Rights Amendment. Its leaders managed to get the prayer-in-school amendment onto the Senate floor (no small feat), but were unable to translate that or much of anything else of substance into victories. Though the New Right supported Ronald Reagan, who convincingly uttered many of its platitudes (it loved, for example, his 1983 "evil empire" speech in Orlando) and who knighted the movement with legitimacy, Reagan did not pursue the New Right's political agenda with the holy zeal that they had expected. He didn't produce a constitutional amendment outlawing abortion, he didn't get legisled prayer into school, he didn't curtail the rights of homosexuals, and he rarely went to church. His successor, blue-blooded Episcopalian George Bush, who has repeated some of the same platitudes as Reagan (though not as convincingly), did even less. And now they face a Clinton White House.

"Some affiliated with the Religious Right," wrote Tom Roberts, "argue that aside from the notable exception of conservative appointments to the judicial system, including the Supreme Court, evangelicals have seen few rewards for their efforts at the polls."[5]

On April 24, 1990, for example, representatives of the Gay and Lesbian Task Force, at the invitation of the White House, stood in the Oval Office for the signing of the "hate crimes"[6] bill. More than a decade after the New Right promised to bring morality to America, George Bush was bringing gays to the White House instead (no doubt Bill Clinton will be bringing in even more)! Obviously, whatever the New Christian Right did in the eighties didn't work.

And, considering their tactics, no wonder. However righteous some of its causes, its methods often weren't, and this made bad press on the evening news. *Christian Voice* published its infamous *Candidate's Biblical Scorecard*, which kept a record of incumbents who failed to register a "pro-biblical vote" on everything from a balanced budget amendment to the Nicaraguan "Freedom Fighters."[7] Fund-raising hysteria, like one letter that warned that donations to this organization "may well be the difference between America surviving and America being destroyed by God's wrath—perhaps through nuclear fire and brimstone,"[8] didn't play well in the press, or in Peoria. Alaska state senator Edna DeVries's comment that non-Christians should "leave the country," or Indiana Moral Majority leader Greg Dixon's prayer "hit list,"[9] or Baptist minister W. A. Criswell's statement that "this notion of separation of church and state was the figment of some infidel's imagination,"[10] turned off many Americans, who still harbor a healthy suspicion of mixing religion and politics. When the New Right's most public figure, Pat Robertson, publicly accused George Bush of engineering Jimmy Swaggart's sexual transgressions in order to discredit Robertson's 1988 presidential campaign, it became obvious that the New Christian Right needed a massive political and public relations overhaul.

"Evangelicals need to become students of the political process," said Robert Dugan, director of the Washington office of the National Association of Evangelicals (NAE). "They need to move to greater sophistication with integrity and knowledge."[11]

They are. Bible-thumpers fresh from the corn patch, breathing hellfire and brimstone against legislators who didn't pass "Bible-based" laws, are slowly being replaced by more politically astute conservatives working behind the scenes to promote the same agenda as the Bible-thumpers but without the hellfire and damnation. "A new cadre has come in now," says Moen, "who have the savvy and sophistication that they were once lacking."

The New Right has toned down the rhetoric too. Jimmy

Swaggart's warning to his political opponents that "you have not set yourself against the so-called moral McCarthyites. You have not set yourself against the hick fundamentalists. You have set yourself against God!"[12] is being replaced with a more sophisticated, less sectarian approach. Instead of calling the abortion struggle a battle to stop "this national Holocaust from bringing down the unmitigated wrath of the Almighty God upon this sin-laden iniquitous nation," it is now a debate over "the rights of the unborn"; school prayer is now "equal opportunity" for religious values; and tuition tax credits have become "freedom of choice" for religious education. They don't as often, at least openly, call positions antithetical to theirs "of the devil." Homosexuals are not as often publicly referred to as "perverts and sodomists." Activists are trained also to avoid the "God-called-me-to-warn-you-in-the-name-of-the-Lord-Jesus-Christ-that-your-political-position-is-against-His-Holy-Word" oratory.

Nevertheless, even now some New Right activists occasionally slip up. In 1992, Jay Grimstead, chairman of the New Right California Activist's Network, mailed a letter to William B. Allen, a political science professor running for the U.S. Senate against conservative darling Bill Dannemeyer. Grimstead warned that "we are calling upon you in the name of Jesus Christ the king of the universe, to immediately step down from this foolish attempt at the Senate seat and to publicly announce that you are throwing your weight and your campaign behind the Dannemeyer effort for victory." If Allen refused to retreat from his "foolish path," this "political abortion that can only aid the forces of darkness," Grimstead warned that besides political consequences, he might face heavenly ones too. "We suspect," he prophesied, "that God Himself will make efforts to discipline you and judge this action of yours however He sees fit. As anyone who has been disciplined by our Heavenly Father can tell you, He can deal very forcibly with us."[13]

Though Grimstead claimed that it was a "rough draft," and later mailed a revision without the threats, the letter revealed that, despite their outward political conversion, the New Right's heart hasn't changed.

Besides replacing the wrath-of-God bombast (with exceptions) for more acceptable terminology, the New Right has revised its overall strategy. Realizing that it can't win in Congress or the White House, at least for now, the New Christian Right has been immersed in a nationwide campaign to *quietly* get involved in local, county, and state politics instead.

"The coming decade of the 90s poses the greatest opportunity for activism at the grassroots," says James Muffett, director of the Michigan Committee for Freedom. "The time has come for us to take our eyes off the White House and focus on the grassroots."[14]

Working mostly through the Republican Party, the New Christian Right is getting people into offices from school boards to state legislatures across the nation.

"Conservative evangelical Christians either run or help run the Republican Party in at least half a dozen states," wrote political analyst Rob Gurwitt, and they "are campaigning for and winning council seats and school board posts from Oregon to Georgia." They have, he said, "developed a group of experienced political strategists who now are surfacing in the campaigns and organizations of mainstream candidates and political groups. The Christian Right is no longer a political innocent. Its leaders have learned how to reach for power."[15]

And they are now reaching in places where it's more likely that they'll get that power too.

"We tried to charge Washington," said Robert Reed, director of Pat Robertson's Christian Coalition, "when we should have been focusing on the states. The real battle of concern to Christians are in neighborhoods, school boards, city councils, and state legislatures."[16]

The key word epitomizing the new approach is *coalition*. Instead of a few highly concentrated power structures centralized in one area, small independent groups are spreading over America and working toward the same goals. "In the nineties," said Tim LaHaye, president of Family Life Seminar and New Right leader, "the Religious Right is going to be composed of a host of independently, locally sponsored and funded organizations that work in unison, but individually."[17]

This guerrilla approach has distinct advantages over conventional warfare. First, you don't need as much political savvy to deal with a school board in Podunk, Arkansas, as with the U.S. Senate in Washington, and therefore the less sophisticated cadres will be able to make an impact in places where previously they couldn't. Most Americans don't know much about local politics, most aren't involved, and most don't even care—an apathy that works to the New Right's advantage. During the 1988 presidential campaign, for example, one poll showed that 49 percent of Americans didn't know that Lloyd Bentsen was Michael Dukakis's running mate!

Voter turnout is usually very low too, another situation the New Right seeks to use to its advantage. "There is no doubt," wrote Dugan of NAE, "that evangelical Christians can win the culture war, by the sheer weight of their vote."[18]

Also, with this low-key approach, independent organizations working at the grass-roots level are not likely to attract as much hostile media attention as did hordes of preachers in Washington shouting Bible verses and declaring, "We're going to take over for Jesus! Hallelujah!" Perhaps the best advantage to this grass-roots, "congregational" approach is that numerous independent groups dispersed over the nation are much harder to track than a few highly visible ones in Washington. "It's going to be difficult," warns Joe Conn of Americans United for Separation of Church and State, "to monitor the activity of so many small organizations."

Recent California local politics epitomize this grass-roots thrust. In the early nineties the New Right wrestled control of half the county Republican Central Committees, as well as the state board. In San Diego County, sixty New Right activists, some running as "stealth candidates,"[19] won seats on the school board, water board, and the city council in November 1990. Conservative evangelicals left over from Pat Robertson's campaign not only remain in the state's Republican structure, but are working to take it over.

"Following the 1988 elections," wrote Frederick Clarkson, "Robertson's cadre took over the California Republican Assembly (CRA), a conservative party unit. The CRA, in alliance with

Young Americans for Freedom, College Republicans and a group of right-wing officials . . . plotted the takeover of the county Republican Committees and ultimately the state board."[20]

Pat Robertson's Christian Coalition (CC), unlike the defunct Moral Majority, is spreading the New Right political gospel at the local level, where it "will promote Christian values through a network of state affiliates and county chapters."[21] Having begun with a mailing list of 1.8 million names left over from Robertson's last presidential gambit, as of this writing the organization claims 250,000 members in forty states, and, according to CC literature, the numbers are growing.

"If the response we are witnessing nationwide is any indication," wrote national field director of CC Guy Rodgers, "Christians everywhere agree that it is time for such excellence [in political power], for the message is spreading like a prairie fire. . . . Christians by the thousands are getting serious about impacting the arena of public policy."[22]

According to Christian Coalition's promotional literature, it plans to represent Christian concerns before local councils, state legislatures, and Congress, as well as training Christian leaders for "effective social and political action." One advertisement reads that "now Christians can unite behind a grass-roots movement that will change the status quo." Another, promoting a two-day Christian Coalition Leadership School, said: "Believe it nor not, the Lord may even want you to run for office." Another reads: "A grass-roots union of Evangelicals, profamily Roman Catholics and their allies, we are determined to redress the plundering of our Judeo-Christian heritage."

Some of its material, especially in the secular press, is savvy, indicative of the New Right's more seasoned approach and Pat Robertson's political maturation. On June 20, 1990, Christian Coalition ran a full-page ad in the *Washington Post* (costing today $44,350), addressed to "the Congress of the United States." In the form of a letter written by Robertson, the ad warned Congress about appropriating tax money for "art" that many Americans find offensive.

"There may be," the ad concluded, "more homosexuals and pedophiles in your district than there are Roman Catholics and

Baptists. You may find the working folks in your district want you to use their money to teach their sons how to sodomize one another. You may find that the Roman Catholics in your district want their money spent on pictures of the Pope soaked in urine.

"But maybe not.

"There is one way to find out.

"Vote for the NEA appropriation just like Pat Williams, John Frohnmayer, and the Gay and Lesbian Task Force want.

"And make my day."

Signed, "Pat Robertson."

Robertson didn't warn about "the wrath of an angry God" falling upon those heathen who voted to promote art done by "unredeemed sodomites and perverts." Nor did he talk about "the demise of our Judeo-Christian civilization" or about a "political holy war between the forces of darkness and of light," so typical of the New Right bombast of the 1980s. Instead, the ad comes across as a forceful, well-reasoned entreaty that would appeal to many conscientious Americans, religious or not, who don't like the idea of $175 million spent for various "art" projects that included, to quote Robertson, "one man urinating in the mouth of another."

The New Right's 1990 moral agenda doesn't differ much from its 1980 one. Now, however—using a more secular tone and basing its tenets, not on wrath-of-God theology, but on simple morality and common sense—the movement can marshal support from many Americans who, while not necessarily agreeing with its religious views, can sympathize with its political ones. You don't have to be a pre-trib-once-saved-always-saved-tongues-speaking-Bible-fundamentalist to not want tax money funding Robert Mapplethorpe homoerotica.

Unquestionably, the most powerful asset the New Right possesses is the moral high ground it has firmly staked out on many positions. Even most people who are prochoice don't *like* abortion, but see it as the best of bad choices. And what responsible citizen, secular or religious, isn't disgusted by the crime, drugs, and moral depravity of our cities? Who isn't concerned about America's schools, youth, morals, and culture? At least the New Right is making a serious effort to deal with these moral concerns, and that effort alone will marshal supporters and power.

"Today ordinary Americans are being stuffed with garbage: by Donahue-Geraldo-Oprah freak shows (crossdressing in the marketplace; skinheads at your corner luncheonette; pop psychologists rhapsodizing over the airways about the minds of serial killers and sex offenders); by Maury Povich news; by 'Hard Copy'; by Howard Stern; by local newscasts that do special segments devoted to hyping hype. Last month, in supposedly sophisticated New York, the country's biggest media market, there ran a craven five-part series on the 11 o'clock news called 'Where Do They Get Those People . . . ?,' a special report on where Geraldo and Oprah and Donahue get their freaks (the promo for the series featured Donahue interviewing a diapered man with a pacifier in his mouth)."[23]

This moral lament about America's media didn't come from Dr. James Dobson on his "Focus on the Family" radio program, but from Watergate reporter Carl Bernstein (not exactly James Dobson) in *The New Republic* (not exactly *Focus on the Family*).

In the late 1980s, after the televangelist scandals, the Ivan-Boesky-Wall-Street shenanigans, Iran Contra, and the Gary Hart–Donna Rice sleaze, self-flagellating articles in national magazines with titles such as "What's Wrong?"[24] or "A Nation of Liars"[25] filled the newsstands. America went through another of its periodic fits of morality that the Europeans find so amusing. But nothing changed. The early nineties have vomited into American laps the Bill Clinton–Gennifer Flowers affair, the S. & L. scandal, Jeffrey Dahmer, the Rodney-King-beating-verdict-riot triptych, and the House bank rip-off.

As long as the New Christian Right not only remonstrates about our moral woes—as does everyone from Jesse Jackson to David Duke—but works full time to remedy them, it will, especially as it matures, become more powerful.

"The strategy against the American radical left," wrote Pat Robertson in a newsletter sent to members of his 700 Club, "should be the same as General Douglas MacArthur employed against the Japanese in the Pacific . . . bypass their strongholds, then surround them, isolate them, bombard them, then blast the individuals out of their power bunkers with hand-to-hand combat. The battle for Iwo Jima was not pleasant, but our troops won it. The battle to regain the soul of America won't be pleasant either, but we will win it!"[26]

Obviously, since his failed 1988 campaign, Robertson has been doing more than praying. Though the New Right has avoided using high-profile leaders like Falwell, as it did in the 1980s, Robertson has taken the mantle. Besides his 700 Club, his law school, his political organizations, and his prosperous business ventures, Robertson manages to release a new book under his name almost yearly. His *The New World Order* (1991), which made the *New York Times* bestseller list, warned about a secret conspiracy involving the Illuminati, the Council of Foreign Relations, the Trilateral Commission, and the United Nations, which are all attempting to "destroy the Christian faith" and "replace it with an occult-inspired world socialist dictatorship" that would include "drunkards, drug dealers, communists, atheists, New Age worshipers of Satan, secular humanists, oppressive dictators, greedy moneychangers, revolutionary assassins, adulterers, and homosexuals."[27]

He also had a section on the Ten Commandments. "The utopians have talked of world order," he wrote. "Without saying so explicitly, the Ten Commandments set the only order that will bring world peace."[28] He then summarized each. At the fourth, he lamented that there are no more religious Sunday laws, but only those that "can be shown to have a clearly secular purpose." He wrote too that "only when people *are permitted* [i.e., blue laws?] to rest from their labors, to meditate upon God, to consider his way, to dream of a better world can there be progress and genuine human betterment."[29]

The book is not without hypocrisy, either. Robertson lamented how American tobacco companies export tobacco around the world, while in America "we're learning about the dangers of tobacco, about lung cancer and emphysema."[30] Meanwhile, under the same cover he bragged about how Christian Coalition saved Jesse Helms—one of the tobacco industry's most potent voices in Washington—from electoral defeat!

In the book, Robertson made himself look like an authority on United States and world history, international finance and banking, international relations, politics, law, and economics (in the bio on the back flap it says that his 700 Club is now suddenly a "news talk program"). *The New World Order* also was sprinkled with references to Pat's numerous accomplishments as "a broadcaster, an author, and longtime follower of and participant in the political process." He said: "In Guatemala City I was personally giving out relief supplies to some eight thousand people. . . . In my 1987 address to the Council on Foreign Relations. . . . In a major address to the national convention of the Republican party in New Orleans, I mentioned. . . . I served in the First Marine Division in Korea under the overall command of General Douglas MacArthur. . . . After the general election I spoke to President Elect Carter. . . . As a former candidate for the presidential nomination of the Republican party. . . . When I met with the then prime minister of Israel. . . ."

Though he hasn't said so publicly, Robertson is probably looking for another presidential gambit, maybe in 1996—and his impressive record, so clearly expressed in *The New World Order*, supposedly refutes charges that he is unqualified.

Another powerful figure in the New Right of the 1990s is Dr. James Dobson. Widely respected among Christians, including Adventists, Dr. Dobson advocates such solid Christian principles regarding family and child rearing that he sounds like Ellen White. His *Focus on the Family* magazine arrives at 1.9 million homes each month (including mine), more homes even than *Parenting* magazine; his first parenting book, *Dare to Discipline*, has so far sold two million copies. His first privately distributed film on child rearing reached sixty million viewers (that's more than saw *Who Framed Roger Rabbit?*). And his radio program, "Focus on the Family," is heard by a million listeners daily on 1,350 outlets. For those interested in applying conservative Christian values to their homes and family, Dr. Dobson is, deservedly, a hero.

He's so popular, in fact, that he has even been urged to run for office, something that he says he will never do. "Eighteen years ago," Dr. Dobson said, "I was talking about the family in the context of society, and that is the limit of my public role now."

Though Dr. Dobson may not be running for office, he has become exceedingly political. Through the Family Research Council, the political lobbying arm of his nationwide Focus on the Family organization, Dobson has immersed himself into New Right politicking. Under the direction of former Reagan domestic policy advisor Gary Bauer, the Family Research Council has grown from two to seventeen workers, and now has chapters in almost twenty states. Unlike many of the New Right organizations of the 1990s, Family Research Council is centered in Washington, D.C., where it "is striving to build an understanding of the pro-family agenda in both the legislative and executive branches of the federal government. . . . From the White House to Capitol Hill, our lobbyists are working to ensure that the needs and values of the family are known and respected."[31]

But even with the Family Research Council focusing on Washington, Dr. Dobson promotes grassroot coalitions around the country. A Religious News Service report headline reads: "Dobson organization aiding formation of pro-family coalitions."[32] Dr. Dobson's own literature states that "many of the major family-related public policy battles are won and lost at state and local levels. Consequently, it is essential that the various activist groups lobbying for traditional values in each state work together to accomplish their goals. With this in mind, Focus on the Family has been actively involved in helping these groups coordinate their efforts through the formation of statewide pro-family coalitions. About half the states already have one of these coalitions in operation: the goal is to develop pro-family coalitions in all 50 states."[33]

As are most other New Right organizations, Dobson's is also working quietly. Focus on the Family spokesman Michael Jameson says Dr. Dobson "doesn't want media scrutiny."[34] Dobson also has been urging followers "to keep secret their participation in the coalition and even that a coalition exists."[35]

"Dobson entered politics quietly," said a rare *Washington Post* profile, "without the press conferences and pomp that surrounded predecessors like the Rev. Jerry Falwell. This reflects the maturing of a certain segment of evangelicals within mainstream politics, particularly in the Republican party."[36]

While the coalition's work is quiet and usually behind the scenes, Dr. Dobson himself has an influential public outreach. "He is available to his followers and believers in virtually every radio market in the United States on a daily basis," said liberal activist lawyer Barry Lynn. "This gives him a tremendous capacity to deliver messages to Congress on specific issues. He can literally launch mailbags of letters to the Congress simply by talking about a piece of legislation on his daily radio program."[37]

Dobson's influence, however, comes more from the sanity of his stances than from his media access, which is minuscule compared to that of his opponents. While Magic Johnson, for instance (whose media access dwarfs Dr. Dobson's), advocates "safe sex," Dobson, along with the New Right, uncompromisingly stresses abstention from *any* sex, safe or not, until marriage, especially when condoms can't guarantee protection. According to Dr. Dobson, not one of eight hundred sexologists attending a recent conference raised a hand when asked if they would trust a thin rubber sheath to protect them during intercourse with a known HIV-infected person. "And yet," Dr. Dobson continued, "they're willing to tell our kids that 'safe sex' is within reach and that they can sleep around with impunity."[38]

Who can argue with that logic? Who wants their children exposed to these risks? And what organizations wielding any substantive influence are advocating abstention from sex until marriage, except the New Right?

Unfortunately, along with the moral high ground they have carved out on these and other issues, the New Right has taken a dangerously low road on individual liberty and freedom of religion. The Adventist scenario of last-day events, clarified in *The Great Controversy*, can happen only when this nation refutes the principles of church-state separation that are embodied in the First Amendment of the U.S. Constitution—principles that the New Right openly wars against!

A newsletter done by Pat Robertson's American Center for Law and Justice (ACLJ) captured the New Right's disdain for the wall of separation between church and state with the headline: "Tear Down This Wall!"[39] The author, Keith Fournier (of the "Evangelical Catholic"), who is now the executive director of Robertson's ACLJ (see the connection?) used the Berlin Wall as an analogy to America's metaphorical one.

"Yet there is a wall," he explained, "which has been mistakenly erected in our own beloved country. Its impact on religious freedom has perhaps had an even more devastating effect. It is the so-called wall of separation of church and state." Fournier then warns that this wall has been used as a "club against the free exercise of religion and religious speech," which have been so hampered in America that Christians might find more religious freedom on "the streets of Moscow" than in the United States.

For this reason—not its warning against "safe sex" or its crusade against abortion or what it might do to the sales of *Playboy*—the New Right poses a threat. The persecution outlined in *The Great Controversy* won't come from militant gays, secular humanists, atheists, or Marxists, but from professed Christians.

"It will be declared," Ellen White wrote, "that men are offending God by the violation of the Sunday Sabbath; that this sin has brought calamities which will not cease until Sunday observance shall be strictly enforced."[40]

Atheists, secular humanists, and liberals won't declare that Sunday-law violators are "offending God." Conservative Christians like those in the New Right—the kind who already blame America's woes on its violation of God's laws—will. Merely replace "violation of the Sunday Sabbath" with "abortion" or "pornography" or "secular humanism" in the above quote, and you have New Right rhetoric today.

"The issue is survival," wrote Jerry Falwell. "If the Scriptures and human history teach us anything, it is that no society that violates Divine principles can long survive."[41] "Ministers who deny the obligation of the divine law," Ellen

White wrote, "will present from the pulpit the duty of yielding obedience to the civil authorities as ordained of God."[42] Their denial comes not from open rejection of the law but of the true Sabbath, which the New Right—despite all its pro–God's law rhetoric—does reject.

"For whosoever shall keep the whole law, and yet offend in one point, he is guilty of all" (James 2:10)—yet all the New Right leaders repudiate the seventh-day Sabbath in favor of Sunday, a day with no biblical sanctity. Most of them have certainly been exposed to the Sabbath truth. Though some will join those who "keep the commandments of God" (Revelation 14:12), most will continue to scorn it. Meanwhile, as it gains political power, the New Right is moving toward a fulfillment of Ellen White's warning of persecution by Christians united with the state.

"As the Protestant churches reject the clear, Scriptural arguments in defense of God's law . . . they are now adopting a course which will lead to the persecution of those who conscientiously refuse to do what the rest of the Christian world are doing, and acknowledge the claims of the papal sabbath."[43]

Non-Adventists see it too. American Civil Liberties Union executive director Ira Glasser warned about those who will "shape America *in their image*—an America dominated by government-imposed religious values."[44] However distasteful the ACLU might be to most Adventists, Glasser described the future perfectly, even prophetically, for "an America dominated by government-imposed religious values" is exactly what *The Great Controversy* warns about. "When the leading churches of the United States, uniting upon such points of doctrine as are held by them in common, shall influence the state *to enforce their decrees and to sustain their institutions*, then Protestant America will have formed an *image* of the Roman hierarchy, and the infliction of civil penalties upon dissenters will inevitably result."[45]

Though the New Right hasn't attained enough clout for this type of persecution to happen yet, it's moving in that direction. This trend was clearly seen at the 1992 Republican National Convention, which, at times, according to one news report, "had the look of a religious revival."[46] The Republicans' stress on family values (admittedly short-lived) came from the influence of the conservative evangelicals within the party structure. "Partisans of the Christian right," wrote *Washington Post* reporter E. J. Dionne, "not only flexed their muscles organizationally and had power beyond their numbers, but also saw Bush's campaign adopt one of their favorite themes, 'traditional family values,' as a rallying point for the fall campaign."[47] *The Wall Street Journal* reported one source as estimating that evangelical conservatives accounted for "as much as 40 percent of the delegates" in Houston.[48] Said New Right activist Martin Mawyer, "If I didn't know any better, I would assume the [Republican Party] platform was written by the religious right."

A few weeks after the Republican convention, Christian Coalition held its Second Annual Road to Victory Conference in Virginia Beach. At the three-day planning and strategy session, which included George Bush as a speaker, Pat Robertson told cheering delegates the last night of the conference that whatever the 1992 election outcome is—"We'll be back in 1993. We'll be back in 1994. We'll be back in 1995. We'll be back in 1996. We'll be back in 1997. We'll be back in 1998. We'll be back in 1999. We'll be back until we win it all!"

Indeed, even before Clinton's electoral landslide, New Right leaders were wondering if it would not be to their advantage for the Democrats to win the White House. That way, if Clinton turns out to be another Jimmy Carter, or worse, the New Right can come back in 1996 with a vengeance, as it did in 1980 with Ronald Reagan, who swept into office in a backlash against Carter. The New Right is already blaming the recent Republican loss on Bush's refusal to follow its agenda. As soon as the 1992 election ended (even before, actually), the New Right set its eyes on 1996. As Robertson said, the conservative Christian agenda will "be back." Take his word on this one.

In one sense, the title, The New Christian Right, is a misnomer: It's neither new (it started in the 1970s) nor so Christian (its tactics have hardly been always Christlike) nor so right (it holds some dangerous views of church-state separation).

What's new is the approach. Like David Duke, who shed his

Ku Klux Klan hood for a three-piece suit and won a seat in the Louisiana state legislature, evangelicals are mastering the game. They now understand, among other things, that publicly threatening the wrath of God on those who support welfare payments to the poor or who object to tuition tax credits just won't cut it in twentieth-century America. They are smarter, more sophisticated, and more tactful than they were in the 1980s, and therefore more dangerous. What this new, low-key, grassroots strategy reveals is that, far from being dead, the New Christian Right— in the lowest sense of the phrase—has been "born again."

1. Pamela Maize Harris, "Did Jerry Falwell Sell Out the Store for Tax-Free Bonds?" See *Liberty*, Sept./Oct. 1991, 2-7.

2. Sidney Blumenthal, "The Righteous Empire," *The New Republic*, 22 Oct. 1984, 18.

3. Thomas Atwood, "Through a Glass Darkly," *Policy Review*, Fall 1990, 44.

4. Quoted in Clifford Goldstein, "The New Christian Right: Born Again?" *Shabbat Shalom*, April-June 1991, 4.

5. Tom Roberts, "Religion in Politics: a lower profile in '92," *Religious News Service*, 14 Feb. 1992, 3.

6. R. Evans and R. Novak, "Bush and the Gay Lobby," *Washington Post*, 25 May 1990.

7. *Candidates' Biblical Scorecard*, Biblical News Service—Christian Voice (Costa Mesa, Calif., 1986).

8. Letter from Robert Grant's "Christian Voice," 1986.

9. William Bole, "Battle escalates over proper place of religion in politics," *Religious News Service*, 1 Aug. 1986, 1.

10. Quoted in Jim Buie, "Praise the Lord and Pass the Ammunition," *Church and State*, October 1984.

11. Quoted in David Aikman, "Washington Scorecard," *Christianity Today*, 21 Oct. 1989, 23.

12. The Jimmy Swaggart Television Program, January 5, 1986.

13. Quoted in *Harper's*, May 1992, 24.

14. "Christian Coalition Expands Across the USA: Christian Activism on the Rise," *Christians' America*, Official Newsletter of the Christian Coalition, Spring 1990.

15. Rob Gurwitt, "The Christian Right Has Gained Political Power. Now What Does It Do?" *Governing*, October 1989, 52.

16. Quoted in "The Christian Coalition: Ganging Up on the First Amendment," *Church and State*, April 1990, 12.

17. Kim Lawton, "Whatever Happened to the Religious Right?" *Christianity Today*, 15 Dec. 1989, 44.

18. Robert Dugan, *Winning the New Civil War* (Portland, Ore.: Multnomah, 1991), 189.

19. A "Stealth Candidate" is one who campaigns for political office on a platform that has wide appeal and does not disclose the right-wing positions that he will adopt once he is in office.

20. Fred Clarkson, "California Dreamin'," *Church and State*, October 1991, 5.

21. From a promotional pamphlet put out by the Christian Coalition, Chesapeake, Virginia.

22. Guy Rodgers, "New Wave of Christian Activists on the Scene," *Christian American*,

March/April 1992, 23.

23. Carl Bernstein, "The Idiot Culture," *The New Republic*, 8 June 1992, 25.

24. *Time*, 25 May 1987, 14.

25. *U.S. News and World Report*, 27 Feb. 1987, 54.

26. *Pat Robertson's Perspective*, April-May 1992, 4.

27. Pat Robertson, *The New World Order* (Dallas: Word Publishing, 1991), 227.

28. Ibid., 233.

29. Ibid., 236.

30. Ibid., 20.

31. From an undated promotional brochure put out by the Family Research Council.

32. "Dobson Organization Aiding the Formation of Pro-Family Coalitions," *Religious News Service,* 24 Feb. 1989, 2.

33. Ibid., 35.

34. Ibid., 2.

35. Ibid., 15.

36. *Washington Post*, 8 Aug. 1990, C3.

37. In "An Interview With the ACLU's Barry Lynn," *Church and State*, July-August 1991, 11.

38. *Focus on the Family* newsletter, 13 Feb. 1992.

39. Keith Fournier, Esq., "Tear Down This Wall!" *Law & Justice*, Winter 1992, 1.

40. *The Great Controversy*, 590.

41. Jerry Falwell, *Listen, America!* (New York: Bantam Books, 1980), prologue.

42. *The Great Controversy*, 592.

43. Ibid.

44. Undated ACLU newsletter.

45. *The Great Controversy*, 445, emphasis supplied.

46. *National and International Religious Report*, 24 Aug. 1992, 1.

47. *Washington Post*, 21 Aug. 1992, A28.

48. *Wall Street Journal*, 20 Aug. 1992, A10.

SEVEN:

New Right Nonsense

A common theme among New Right leaders is how our nation needs to return to the good old days when godliness reigned.

"By relearning the facts that a righteous new government came from a righteous people seeking to advance the kingdom of Christ," wrote Dr. James Kennedy, "it will be possible to reverse the ungodly laws of this generation."[1]

"We must reestablish," wrote Franky Schaeffer, "the beauty and fullness in love of a Christian nation that was once ours."[2]

"I invite you," wrote Pat Robertson, "to join a growing army of Christian patriots working to win America back to God."[3]

"Let me point out," wrote Tim LaHaye, "that for 150 years this nation was built on biblical principles that assured freedom, community decency, and domestic tranquility."[4]

"It is shocking," wrote Robert Dugan, "to realize how far our nation has drifted from its historic respect for the God-given right to life."[5]

"God blessed this nation because in its early days she sought to honor God and the Bible, the inerrant word of the living God," wrote Jerry Falwell. "Any diligent student of American history finds that our great nation was founded by godly men upon godly principles to be a Christian nation."[6]

One wonders just what those "godly principles" were. Were they found in the uprooting and massacre of thousands upon thousands of Native Americans by "a righteous people seeking to advance the kingdom of God"? Were they in the enslavement of millions of black Africans upon whose raging sweat and spilled blood this "Christian nation" was built? Or were they in the persecution of religious dissenters in the early days, when America "sought to honor God and the Bible"? Or maybe they were best seen in the millions of children forced to work up to sixteen hours a day in hot factories, where sometimes they would stumble into machines that tore off their limbs or killed them?

The most eloquent statement about America's glorious Christian past—when it "was built on biblical principles that assured freedom, community decency, and domestic tranquility"— came from one who experienced those principles firsthand, former slave Frederick Douglass:

> What, to the American slave, is your 4th of July? I answer; a day that reveals to him, more than all other days in the year, the gross injustice and cruelty to which he is the constant victim. To him your celebration is a sham . . . . your prayers and hymns, your sermons and thanksgivings, with all your religious parade and solemnity, are, to him, mere bombast, fraud, deception, impiety and hypocrisy—a thin veil to cover up crimes which would disgrace a nation of savages. There is not a nation on the earth guilty of practices more shocking than are the people of the United States. . . . You can bare your bosom to the storm of British artillery to throw off a three-penny tax on tea; and yet wring the last hard-earned farthing from the grasp of the black laborers of your country. You profess to believe that "of one blood, God made all nations of men to dwell on the face of all the earth" (Acts 17:16), and hath commanded all men everywhere to love one another; yet you notoriously hate (and glory in your hatred) all men whose skins are not colored like your own. . . . The existence of slavery in this country brands your republicanism a sham, your humanity a base pretense, and your Christianity a lie.[7]

Another writer expressed the Lord's view of America during

slavery: "Human agony is carried from place to place and bought and sold. Angels have recorded it all; it is written in the book. The tears of the pious bondmen and bondwomen, of fathers, mothers, and children, brothers and sisters, are all bottled up in heaven. God will restrain his anger but little longer. His wrath burns against this nation and especially against the religious bodies that have sanctioned this terrible traffic and have themselves engaged in it."[8]

Now as bad as abortion, pornography, and television are today (and they *are* bad), are we supposed to believe that— despite the slavery, oppression, and outright murder that characterized this nation's early years—God blessed America then, but He is *only now* about to unleash His wrath because of *Roe v. Wade*, phone sex, and Murphy Brown's illegitimate baby?

No question, America's *personal* moral values have declined, but this reflects a failure of preachers more than of politicians. The solution is not to put born-again Christians in office, but to have born-again Christians in our homes and churches, where our nation's character is formed one soul at a time. The New Right's attempt at salvation by legislation reveals, not a revival of Christian godliness in our nation, but the absence of it. "We as Christians," wrote conservative Christian leader John Whitehead, "share a major responsibility for what has happened, since a significant factor has been the dwindling influence of Christianity, which has allowed humanistic thought to rise and dominate."[9]

Gallup polls reveal that, despite the large numbers on the church books, American Christianity reflects Jimmy Swaggart more than it does Christ. Church involvement, said George Gallup, "does not seem to make a great deal of difference in the way we live our lives." Even more appalling, his polls show that the churched in this country are "just as likely as the un- churched to engage in unethical behavior."[10] If, a century ago, Ellen White in *The Great Controversy* could write that "the line of distinction between professed Christians and the ungodly is now hardly distinguishable,"[11] what would she say about today?

Jesus hasn't failed Christians; they have failed Him, and what they can't accomplish through their impotent preachers and teachers, they want secular law to do for them instead.

"When the early church became corrupted by departing from the simplicity of the gospel and accepting heathen rites and customs," wrote Ellen White in *The Great Controversy*, "she lost the Spirit and power of God; and in order to control the consciences of the people, she sought the support of the secular power. The result was the papacy, a church that controlled the power of the state and employed it to further her own ends, especially for the punishment of 'heresy.' In order for the United States to form an image of the beast, *the religious power must so control the civil government that the authority of the state will also be employed by the church to accomplish her own ends*"[12]— exactly what the New Right seeks to do.

"What Christians have got to do is take back this country, one precinct at a time, one neighborhood at a time, one state at a time," says Robert Reed of Christian Coalition. "I honestly believe that in my lifetime we will see a country once again governed by Christians."[13]

Since when was this nation ever governed specifically by Christians? Almost all the presidents professed some faith, but that hardly made them Christian. Some were boozers, adulterers, and even one (heaven forbid!) a Unitarian. Richard Nixon—when he was illegally bombing Cambodia, spying on his political opponents, and asserting that "I am not a crook" (when he really was)—claimed to be Christian. How many presidents were born again in the radical, life-changing sense that Jesus Himself taught? The truest believer in the White House in decades, Jimmy Carter, was tossed out (with the help of the New Right) and replaced with a man who rarely went to church and whose wife allowed an astrologer to plan part of his itinerary. And despite New Right revisionist history that tries to baptize them into evangelicalism, few of the founding fathers were the Christians about whom Reed fantasizes.

In its earliest days, even before the disestablishment of religion, America had more unchurched people than any other land in Christendom. "In Georgia," wrote Baptist educator and church leader Dr. William Keucher, "at the time of the second Constitutional Convention, fewer than 500 people appeared on the church rolls. A mission society in Europe discussed missionary needs and opportunities in North Carolina in the same paragraph with the appalling needs in India and China."[14]

According to historian Robert Handy in *A Christian America*, the situation in the beginning of the eighteenth century "did not seem favorable for the churches of America. . . . Probably less than 10 percent of the population in the United States were church members in 1800." And though many people not on the church books were still involved with the churches, the "picture was not," Handy wrote, "very promising."[15]

In contrast, more than 40 percent of Americans today attend church weekly (as opposed to 14 percent in Great Britain and 12 percent in France). More Americans go to church in any week than to all sports events combined. Ninety percent of Americans believe in the existence of God. And over 90 percent pray some time in the week.[16]

"Technology, urbanization, social mobility, universal education, high living standards—" wrote Gary Wills, "all were supposed to eat away at religion, in a wash of overlapping acids. But each has crested over America, proving itself a solvent or a catalyst in other areas, but showing little power to corrode or diminish religion. The figures are staggering. Poll after poll confirms them."[17] Indeed, Americans might be professing faith more now than in our "Christian" past.

"We feel that a careful study of the facts of history," wrote three evangelicals in a book that debunks the myth of a Christian America, "shows that early America does not deserve to be considered uniquely, distinctly or even predominately Christian, if we mean by the word *Christian* a state of society reflecting the ideals presented in Scripture. There is no lost golden age to which American Christians may return."[18]

Nevertheless, for Robertson, LaHaye, and Kennedy, America's "Christian" past is part of their blueprint for its "Christian" future. Thus we need to *return* to godliness, to *restore* Christian values, and *reestablish* biblical principles in government, or else face God's retributive judgments—though it would seem that a righteous God would be more likely to judge a nation that kills its born than one that kills its unborn, and that if His divine indignation hadn't struck after centuries of slavery, we're not about to face it after a few decades of *Playboy*.

This myth of America's Christian past is just one of numerous New Right revisionist histories of America. Another is the notion that the founding fathers were orthodox Christians.

"The overwhelming majority of the Founding Fathers of this nation," wrote Tim LaHaye, "were raised and believed in the Christian faith."[19] The argument then proceeds that, because they were Christians, they couldn't have meant for the Constitution to be hostile to religion, as LaHaye and others claim that strict separationism (the idea that the government should remain neutral toward religion and not support it) has made the document anti-religion. Rather, the founding fathers, because they were Christians, would have been accommodationists, argues LaHaye, allowing the government to support religion as long as it didn't favor one church over another.

"This argument about the supposed faith of the Founders," said church-state expert Dr. Stan Hastey, "has become common currency among those seeking to use the state either to fund or to promote religion."[20]

What's ironic about this approach, however, is that by stressing the supposed Christianity of these former leaders, the New Right weakens its argument for government accommodation of religion. The founding fathers—those who allegedly "believed in the Christian faith"—fervently supported what James Madison called "the total separation of the Church from the State."[21] Therefore, the more holy, pious, and Christian the New Right makes the founding fathers, the weaker their argument; otherwise, why did those religious Christians who founded the nation hold views of church-state separation that the New Right teaches are hostile to religion?

Few would challenge the choice of George Washington, Benjamin Franklin, Thomas Jefferson, and James Madison as foremost among the men influencing church-state relationships in our emerging country. They include the "Father of Our Country," three presidents, and the author of the First Amendment. They are also commonly cited by those seeking governmental support, both financial or moral, for religion in America, the kind of support that will ultimately lead to the Sunday legislation described in *The Great Controversy.*

Stories about George Washington's piety are as woven into American tradition as stars and stripes are into Old Glory. Pat Robertson, in his book *America's Dates With Destiny*, devotes a chapter to Washington's Christianity. He said that Washington was "a Christian whose faith in God and respect for God's Word were the central pillars of his public policy."[22] Tim LaHaye, in his book *Faith of Our Founding Fathers*, stressed Washington's prayer life, stringent Bible study, and Christian devotion. "That President George Washington was a devout believer in Jesus Christ," wrote LaHaye, "and accepted Him as His Lord and Savior, is easily demonstrated by a reading of his personal prayer book."[23]

Commenting on Washington's prayers, John Eidsmoe, a legal historian and a religion professor, in a book called *Christianity and the Constitution*, wrote that "these are the sentiments of an Orthodox Christian."[24]

Ben Franklin, whom Eidsmoe referred to as a "so-called deist"[25] (though a "thorough deist" is what Franklin called himself), is also portrayed in the most religious light possible. Eidsmoe classified him as a "secular Puritan"[26] (something like "Christian porn"?). Downplaying the stories of Franklin's amours with the coquettes of the French court, Eidsmoe wrote that "there is no shred of evidence that Franklin had affairs with French women."[27] LaHaye wrote that Franklin had "a definite belief in a sovereign and personal God, gave credence to Bible reading and prayer, and held a deep commitment to the traditional and moral values of the churches of his day."[28] Though he admits that no evidence exists that Franklin ever became a Christian, LaHaye says that "he was extremely respectful of Christianity and never hostile to it."[29]

Thomas Jefferson, of course, is more difficult to baptize. Though LaHaye dismisses him as a "closet Unitarian who had nothing to do with the founding of our nation," Eidsmoe sees Jefferson as a religious man who was not a true deist—that is, he did not believe that God had disassociated Himself from the affairs of men. After quoting Jefferson about God enlightening the minds of men, guiding in their councils, and prospering their measures, Eidsmoe writes: "These are not the words of a deist. Nor would a deist speak of submission to God the way Jefferson did."[30] Eidsmoe stressed that Jefferson read the Bible diligently in English, French, Latin, and Greek, and believed that God not only created the universe but was active in human affairs. "Jefferson probably did not consider himself a Christian before the 1790s," wrote Eidsmoe, but he quotes Jefferson as later saying that "I am a real Christian, that is to say, a disciple of the doctrines of Jesus."[31]

James Madison, too, is portrayed as a Christian. "Because he was a very private man," wrote LaHaye, "and did not believe that government should provide a platform for religious discourse, his early life provides us with the best evidence of his Christian faith."[32] Eidsmoe quotes from Madison sources in order to prove the Christian influence in his life and political philosophy. He says even that Madison's famous *Memorial and Remonstrance*, "far from being an anti-Christian statement, was possibly the closest Madison came to publicly affirming Christianity."[33] Eidsmoe wrote, too, that "nothing in Madison's life or writing suggests that he became disillusioned with Christianity, rejected the fundamental doctrines of the Christian faith, or lost interest in religion."[34]

Whether LaHaye's or Eidsmoe's or Robertson's claims regarding the founding fathers is correct is not the issue. The issue is that the New Right uses this argument to promote accommodation of religious institutions and values, even though in reality making Christians out of the founding fathers undermines the New Right's position on accommodation.

If George Washington had been such a devout Christian, he certainly would not have been hostile to Christianity. Yet in 1789, some Presbyterian elders protested to Washington that the Constitution was too secular and that it lacked any explicit recognition "of the only true God and Jesus Christ, whom he hath sent."[35] Washington dismissed their charge, calmly replying that "the path of true piety is so plain as to require but little political direction."[36]

This "orthodox Christian" told the elders what strict separationists have been saying for years: that the government has no business promoting religion. In those few simple words, Washington displayed an understanding of the basic principle of religious freedom: that church and state need to be separate and that religion does not need "political direction"—a view that the New Right vehemently rejects. This man, whom LaHaye said would "freely identify with [today's] evangelical Christianity,"[37] even negotiated a peace treaty with Tripoli that said, "The United States of America is not in any sense founded upon the Christian religion."

Those today who adhere to principles similar to Washington's are damned as secular humanists, infidels, atheists, and commies. Under which of these headings shall we put George Washington, LaHaye's "devout believer in Jesus"?

What about Benjamin Franklin? This man, whom LaHaye called a "strong advocate of religious freedom," made the oft-quoted statement: "When religion is good, I conceive that it will support itself; and when it does not support itself, and God does not take care to support it, so that its professors are obliged to call for the help of civil powers, 'tis a sign, I apprehend, of it being a bad one."

Those pushing for state-sponsored prayer and Bible reading in school, who want tax dollars to fund their religious enterprises, who want religious symbols placed on public property, who want Sunday blue laws, and who claim that government should support religion, are what Franklin called "professors [who] are obliged to call for the help of civil powers." Franklin understood the basic principle underlying church-state separation: that religion should not *need* state support, unless, of course, as Franklin wrote, it is "a bad one."

According to Eidsmoe, even Thomas Jefferson "approved of Christianity's positive influence on society as a whole." If so, then why did he, in the first year of his presidency, reject the request from a group of Baptists in Danbury, Connecticut, to set aside a day of fasting so that the nation could more readily heal from the wounds of a bitter presidential campaign? Isn't that action hostile to Christianity? Even worse, in that letter, Jefferson even used that perfidious wall-of-separation-between-church-

and-state metaphor, a phrase as hateful to the New Right as *sola Scriptura* was to sixteenth-century Catholics.

Jefferson, who opposed not only any type of general tax for religion (he called it "sinful and tyrannical"), but also taxing a man even for his own faith, observed that "forcing him to this or that teacher of his own religious persuasion, is depriving him of the comfortable liberty of giving his contributions to the particular pastor"[38] whom he chooses. Jefferson was an adamant separationist who understood that religion should not need state support. "It is error alone," he wrote, "which needs the support of the government. Truth can stand by itself."[39]

Those pushing similar separationist views today are branded as "anti-Christian" or "anti-God." Yet these positions were held by a man who, according to Eidsmoe, "saw the value of Christianity for the nation and the individual; [who] attended church, gave to the support of several churches, and lived a pious life"?[40]

James Madison, who (according to LaHaye) had "Christian faith," was not only against tax exemption for churches (even most strict separationists today don't go *that* far), he even opposed the appointment of chaplains to Congress and the military, calling a chaplainship to Congress "a palpable violation of equal rights, as well as Constitutional principles." This man, who wrote the First Amendment, vetoed a bill that would have given the Baptist Church land, saying that it "comprises a precedent for the appropriation of funds of the United States for the use and support of religious societies."[41] And though Eidsmoe called Madison's *Memorial and Remonstrance* "the closest Madison came to publicly affirming Christianity," the document's purpose was to forbid taxes for churches!

Obviously, an inconsistency exists in the New Right's accommodationism. Those opposed to tax dollars for religious education (the same principle that prompted Madison's *Memorial and Remonstrance*) or to laws that would promote sectarian exercises of religion (i.e., Jefferson's refusal to proclaim fast days) or who oppose religious symbols on government property (i.e., Washington's reply to the Presbyterian elders)—are now attacked by the New Right as hostile to Christianity.

But what about the framers of this nation, men who with few exceptions promoted the same strict separationist principles as those who are today branded "anti-Christian"? (Madison, under pressure, reluctantly proclaimed "absolutely indiscriminate" and "merely recommendatory" days of fasting and prayer.) To be consistent, the New Right should brand Jefferson, Madison, Washington, and Franklin, not as religious men, but as a brood of liberal, anti-Christian secular humanist Bolsheviks—which, of course, it does not do.

Instead, it will continue to use the lie about the founding fathers' religious beliefs to promote the lie of its accommodationist agenda, and millions of Americans will continue to believe both.

The New Right has another ploy to rewrite American history to fit its political agenda. This deals with the Establishment Clause of the First Amendment, which reads, "Congress shall make no law respecting an establishment of religion. . . ." Though the meaning seems clear enough, that "Congress shall make *no* law respecting an establishment of religion" (not doing anything to establish religion at all), the New Right and others say that it means only that Congress can't favor one religion over another, but that it can accommodate all religions equally.

"There are many Supreme Court cases," wrote Keith Fournier, "which explicitly affirm that the government must not only tolerate but affirmatively accommodate religion in America."[42]

Chief justice of the United States Supreme Court William H. Rehnquist agrees, saying that the Establishment Clause merely "forbade the establishment of a national religion and forbade preference among religious sects or denominations." But it did not, he said, "prohibit the federal government from providing non-discriminatory aid to religion."[43]

Who's correct?

Because James Madison wrote the Establishment Clause, he should know what it meant—and, fortunately, he left a document that reveals his view on the subject. Also, because "Virginia provided the rationale and the preliminary draft for the First Amendment and its later interpretation,"[44] its history can help us today understand the meaning of the religion clauses.

In Virginia, after the Revolutionary War, state leaders were concerned that moral conditions had deteriorated and that "Lewdness, Wickedness, and Vice" were spreading rapidly. To counter these trends, Patrick Henry, then the most popular politician in Virginia, wrote a bill for the General Assessment of religion, which consisted of a property tax to support the churches. Each taxpayer could determine for himself which church the money went to, and if he didn't choose a specific denomination, the money would go to build church schools. The bill, introduced in 1784, was specifically "for the support of and maintenance of several Ministers and Teachers of the Gospel who are of *different persuasions and Denominations*" and for the upkeep of their churches. In the case of Quakers and "Mennonists," which had no clergy, the money would go in a general fund "to promote their particular mode of worship." In short, Henry's General Assessment was an eighteenth-century version of what the twentieth-century accommodationists believe the First Amendment allows: nonpreferential and nondiscriminatory government aid to all religion.

James Madison went ballistic. First, he successfully conspired to get Patrick Henry out of the State House, where his fiery and powerful oratory mustered support for the General Assessment, and into the governor's chair, where he was out of the fray. Madison then delayed the vote, giving himself time to rally forces against it and write his famous *Memorial and Remonstrance*.

"We remonstrate against this said Bill," he wrote in the closing line of the first paragraph, and then began each of the next fifteen paragraphs with a "Because" that listed his reasons for opposing the General Assessment.

"Because," he said, this bill constituted a "dangerous abuse of power" that threatened their most basic freedoms.

"Because," he said, fifteen centuries of "ecclesiastical establishments" had given birth to superstition, bigotry, and persecution, and this bill could do the same. "Who does not see," he warned, "that the same authority which can establish Christianity, in exclusion of all other Religions, may establish with the same ease any particular sect of Christians, in exclusion of all other Sects?"

"Because the establishment proposed by the Bill is not a requisite for the support of the Christian Religion. To say that it is, is a contradiction to the Christian Religion itself, for every page of it disavows a dependence on the powers of this world."

So alarmed was Madison at this "first experiment with our liberties" that he compared it to the Spanish Inquisition! "Distant as it may be in its present form from the Inquisition, it differs from it only in degree. The one is the first step, the other the last in the career of intolerance."

These were the sentiments of the man who seven years later wrote the Establishment Clause, and yet somehow people construe the clause to allow government aid to religion?

Comparing poor Henry's little bill that wanted only some tax dollars for "different persuasions and religions" to the Inquisition might seem a bit much, but the rhetoric and fervor reveal that Madison understood the most basic principle of religious freedom: that the government must be kept from either hindering or promoting religion. "There is not a shadow of a right," he wrote in another place, "for the general government to intermeddle with religion."[45]

"It is therefore unreasonable, even fatuous," wrote constitutional scholar Leonard Levy, "to believe that an express prohibition of power—'Congress shall make no law respecting an establishment of religion'—vests or creates the power, previously non-existent, of supporting religion by aid to all groups."[46]

In a 1988 book, Joel Hunter showed rare sensitivity on the issues for a New Right activist: "Institutional expression is not without force. As has been mentioned, the power of government and its various institutions is force. . . . And all activities carried on by governmental institutions can't help but convey the force linked with governmental institutions. To believe otherwise is amazingly naive."[47]

Apparently, most New Right activists are either "amazingly naive" or callously indifferent to the potential consequences of their drive to destroy the wall of church-state separation. Or, even more frightening: they know what destruction of the wall can do—and that's what they want.

"The 'image of the beast,'" wrote Ellen White in *The Great Controversy*, "represents that form of apostate Protestantism which will be developed when the *Protestant churches shall seek the aid of the civil power for the enforcement of their dogmas.*"[48] This is exactly what the New Right, by attacking church-state separation, is attempting.

Though the New Right hasn't succeeded yet, it (or some group like it) will. We don't need prophecy to see it coming, either. We need merely to look at the courts. Why? Because for our prophetic scenario as pictured in Revelation and *The Great Controversy* to happen, the courts must revamp their position on the First Amendment.

As the next chapter shows, they're already doing it.

1. Foreword to Catherine Millard, *The Rewriting of America's History* (Camp Hill, Penn.: Horizon House, 1991).

2. Franky Schaeffer, *A Time for Anger: The Myth of Neutrality* (Westchester, Ill.: Crossway, 1982), 78.

3. Christian Coalition promotional letter written by Pat Robertson, 1 Jan. 1992.

4. Tim LaHaye, *Faith of Our Founding Fathers* (Brentwood, Tenn.: Wolgemuth & Hyatt, 1987), 190.

5. Robert Dugan, *Winning the New Civil War* (Portland, Ore.: Multnomah, 1991), 175.

6. Jerry Falwell, *Listen, America!* (New York: Bantam, 1980), 25.

7. Frederick Douglass, Benjamin Quarles, ed. (Englewood Cliffs, N. J.: Prentice Hall, 1968), 46-48.

8. Ellen G. White, *Early Writings* (Washington, D.C.: Review and Herald, 1945), 275.

9. John Whitehead, *The Second American Revolution* (Elgin, Ill.: David C. Cooke Publishing, 1982), 19.

10. "Most Christians Don't Know or Act Their Faith, Gallup Says," *Religious News Service*, 10 May 1990, 10.

11. *The Great Controversy*, 588.

12. Ibid., 443, emphasis supplied.

13. "Robertson's New Coalition Growing in Money and Membership," *Religious News Service*, 15 May 1989, 1.

14. William F. Keucher, "Myths: They Must Be Confronted Before They Distort the Realities of Today," *Liberty*, July/August 1992, 7.

15. Robert Handy, *A Christian America* (New York: Oxford University Press, 1981), 27, 28.

16. George Gallup and Jim Castelli, *The People's Religion* (New York: MacMillan, 1989), 33,

48. Quoted in Gary Wills, *Under God: Religion and American Politics* (New York: Simon & Schuster, 1990), 16.

17. Ibid.

18. Mark Noll, Nathan Hatch, and George Marsden, *The Search for Christian America* (Colorado Springs: Helmers and Howard, 1989), 16.

19. Tim LaHaye, *Faith of Our Founding Fathers*, xi.

20. Quoted in Clifford Goldstein, "Faith of Our Fathers," *Liberty*, January/February 1989, 11.

21. Letter to Robert Walsh from James Madison, 2 Mar. 1819. Quoted in Robert S. Alley, *James Madison on Religious Liberty* (Buffalo: Prometheus, 1985), 81.

22. Pat Robertson, *America's Dates With Destiny* (New York: Thomas Nelson, 1986), 115.

23. LaHaye, 110.

24. John Eidsmoe, *Christianity and the Constitution* (Grand Rapids, Mich.: Baker Book House, 1987), 131.

25. Ibid., 208.

26. Ibid., 191.

27. Ibid., 207.

28. LaHaye, 116.

29. Ibid., 115.

30. Eidsmoe, 228.

31. Ibid., 240.

32. LaHaye, 129.

33. Eidsmoe, 107.

34. Ibid., 100.

35. Quoted in Edwin S. Gaustad, *Faith of Our Fathers* (San Francisco: Harper and Row, 1987), 78.

36. Ibid.

37. LaHaye, 113.

38. *A Bill for Establishing Religious Freedom*, 1777.

39. Thomas Jefferson, *Notes on the State of Virginia*, ed. William Peden (New York: Norton, 1982), 160.

40. Eidsmoe, 245.

41. Quoted in Gaustad, 51.

42. Keith Fournier, "Tear Down This Wall!" *Law & Justice*, Winter 1992, 4.

43. Quoted in Leonard Levy, *The Establishment Clause* (New York: MacMillan, 1986), xii.

44. Thomas Buckley, *Church and State in Revolutionary Virginia, 1776-1787* (Richmond: University of Virginia Press, 1977), iv.

45. Quoted in Robert S. Alley, *James Madison on Religious Liberty* (Buffalo: Prometheus Books, 1985), 71.

46. Leonard Levy, 84.

47. Joel Hunter, *Prayer, Politics, and Power* (Wheaton, Ill.: Tyndale House, 1988), 37.

48. *The Great Controversy*, 445, emphasis supplied.

EIGHT:

H.R. 2797

Walking south from Union Station, I came to the north entrance of Capitol Hill. Police at the security checkpoint used mirrors on the end of long silver handles to snoop under vehicles; others, in gray jumpsuits, handled German shepherds that sniffed each car before the police allowed it entrance. On each side of the checkpoint, cement flower pots the size of hot tubs served as blockades against truck bombers.

I walked between the flowered barriers, along with dozens of other people who poured onto the courtyard, which stretched for the length of about three football fields across the front of the Capitol, which glistened in the May sun like an ancient Mediterranean fantasy. Shirtless, mohawked marines in tight green shorts jogged amid men and women in business suits, crowds with name tags pinned on their lapels gathered on the Capitol steps to be photographed, a red-and-white Coke truck parked by a service entrance, and police politely ordered people onto the sidewalk.

On the south side of the Capitol, off a side street, I entered the Rayburn Building. Having passed through an airportlike metal detector, I walked along the white marble floors, took an elevator to the second level, and then came to room 2237, where the Subcommittee on Civil and Constitutional Rights of the House Judiciary Committee was about to begin. Inside, I met other Adventist religious liberty representatives who were there to lobby in favor of the bill being debated that May morning before the subcommittee: H.R. 2797—otherwise known as The Religious Freedom Restoration Act of 1991.

The what Restoration Act?

Most people weren't aware that religious freedom needed to be restored. Nevertheless, the name was appropriate, and the story behind H.R. 2797 reveals not only how fragile our freedoms are, but also how quickly *The Great Controversy's* scenario about America repudiating its principles of religious freedom could happen.

As with most free exercise issues today, this drama began with a religious minority—those who have unconventional religious practices but whose numbers are not enough to wield the electoral clout needed to protect those practices.

Like Adventists.

This case centered on Alfred Smith, seventy, a Klamath Indian and member of the Native American Church. In the 1970s, this former alcoholic started working as a drug rehabilitation counselor for the Council on Alcohol and Drug Abuse Prevention (ADAPT) in Oregon. When hired, he signed the standard contract stipulating that he would not use alcohol or illegal drugs.

About the same time, Smith began delving into ancient Native American customs, such as the Sioux sun dance, sweat lodges, and other ceremonies that were part of his "spiritual quest," which included eating peyote, an act of worship and communion that goes back more than fourteen centuries for Native Americans. Twenty-four states have exempted Native Americans who use peyote in religious ceremonies from drug laws. Though Oregon, at the time Smith signed the contract, did not exempt ritual peyote use (it does now), Smith thought that his contract did.

It didn't, and ADAPT fired him. When he and another Native American, Galen Black, fired for the same reason, applied for unemployment benefits, the Oregon Employment Division denied their claims on the grounds that the two men lost their jobs for "misconduct connected with work." Smith and Black appealed the decision, arguing that because their use of peyote was religiously motivated, the state could not constitutionally deny their claim. An Oregon appeals court reversed the Employment decision, and four years after Smith and Black lost their jobs, the Oregon Supreme Court ruled that the Free Exercise Clause of the First Amendment protected the ceremonial use of peyote. State officials appealed the ruling to the U.S. Supreme Court, which, after sending the case back to the state one time, finally agreed to hear *Employment Division v. Smith*.

When the 6-3 vote against Smith was announced in 1990, groups on all ends of the political and religious spectrum, from the conservative Christian Rutherford Institute to the ACLU, the American Muslim Council to the National Council of Jewish Women, the Home School Legal Defense Association to People for the American Way—all denounced the ruling.

The National Council of Churches called it "a decision of disastrous consequences."[1] The American Jewish Congress termed it "devastating to the free exercise rights of all Americans, particularly those of minority faith."[2] Representative Stephen J. Solarz (D-N.Y.) said that "with the stroke of a pen, the Supreme Court virtually removed religious freedom—our first freedom—from the Bill of Rights."[3] Forest Montgomery of the National Association of Evangelicals said that the decision "has gutted the Free Exercise Clause of the First Amendment."[4] Bemoaning the decision, David L. Miller, editor of *The Lutheran*, said that "the biggest loser may be American society. The soul of the nation is at stake."[5] Even Associate Justice Sandra Day O'Connor, who agreed with the outcome of *Smith*, said that the court's rationale for making its decision "is incompatible with our nation's fundamental commitment to individual religious liberty" and denigrates the "very purpose of the Bill of Rights."

All this over a Supreme Court decision that refused unemployment benefits to a Native American fired for using peyote?

Not quite. The real issue was not the decision, which was arguably bad, but the majority opinion written by Justice Antonin Scalia, which *undeniably* was. Scalia took the protection of religious freedom away from the courts and placed it in the hands of voters and legislatures—not exactly the safest place, especially for minority faiths.

"We now face," said Representative Solarz, "the grim prospect of popular referenda to determine which religious practices will be protected and which will not. Religion will be subject to the standard interest-group politics that affect our many decisions. It will be the stuff of postcard campaigns, thirty-second spots, scientific polling, and legislative horse trading."[6]

With *Smith*, America has digressed a long way from the time when the Supreme Court recognized that the purpose of the Bill of Rights was to "withdraw certain subjects from the vicissitudes of political controversy, to place them beyond the reach of the majorities and officials." Before *Smith*, the court said that certain rights, including freedom of worship, "may not be submitted to a vote" nor depend on "the outcome of elections."[7] Now, as Justice Scalia admitted in *Smith*, "It may be fairly said that leaving accommodation [of certain religious practices] to the political process will place at a relative disadvantage those religious practices that are not widely engaged in."[8]

What did *Smith* do?

The big question concerning the Free Exercise Clause of the First Amendment is, To what extent does the Bill of Rights protect the free exercise of religion? "The Free Exercise Clause," said the Court years ago, "embraces two concepts—freedom to believe and freedom to act. The first is absolute, but in the nature of things, the second cannot be."[9]

Why not? Because not everything done under the rubric of religion should be protected by the First Amendment. Suppose a cult arose that followed the ancient Canaanite practice of child sacrifice, or the Hindu one of suttee (burning wives on funeral pyres). No court in the land would allow it to engage in those actions, no matter how firmly rooted or sincerely held the religious tradition was. Though polygamy, for instance, was an integral part of Mormonism, the courts would not allow the practice because "the State has a perfect right to prohibit polygamy, and all other open offenses against the enlightened sentiment of mankind, not-withstanding the pretense of religious conviction by which they are advocated or practiced."[10]

Yet should all religious practices against the "enlightened sentiment of mankind" be proscribed, or is not the whole purpose of the Free Exercise Clause to protect practices deemed offensive by the majority? Should the Court differ between suttee and the ritual use of peyote? When and how should the courts draw the line?

By the 1940s, the Supreme Court deemed freedom of religion a "fundamental right"—preferred and precious—and one that required extensive protection, more than, for example, freedom of contract or economic freedom. The Court began veering toward the "strict scrutiny" test of any government burden of a fundamental right, such as religious practice. The government had to face strict scrutiny by the courts if it denied an exemption to someone whose religious beliefs conflicted with a law.

An Adventist Sabbath case in 1963 helped crystallize the strict scrutiny standard. In a situation much like Smith's, Seventh-day Adventist Adele Sherbert lost her job because she refused to work on Sabbath when her South Carolina plant changed from a five- to a six-day work week. Because her refusal was deemed misconduct, she was denied unemployment benefits (though South Carolina allowed benefits to those fired for refusing Sunday work).

The case made it to the U.S. Supreme Court, which voted in her favor. In the majority opinion, written by Justice William Brennan, the Court ruled that a person may not be forced to choose between allegiance to sincerely held religious beliefs and the receipt of generally available governmental benefits, such as unemployment compensation. He also enunciated the concept of "compelling state interest," which means that the state must show why a certain religious practice, for the good of the community, should be forbidden. This idea was applied even before *Sherbert v. Verner* (such as in the Mormon polygamy cases), which merely helped codify it as a legal principle in free exercise cases.

The genius of the "compelling state interest" test, and what made it such a good (though not perfect) protector of religious freedom, was that the burden of proof rested on the *government* to demonstrate why a fundamental right such as the free exercise of religion should not be allowed.

"The Constitution," said legal scholar Douglas Laycock, "does not say that government may prohibit free exercise for compelling reasons. Rather, the Constitution says absolutely that there shall be 'no law' prohibiting free exercise. The implied exception is based on necessity, and its rationale runs no further than cases of clear necessity."[11] The Court deemed that "only the gravest abuses, endangering paramount interests, give occasion for permissible limitation,"[12] and that "only those interests of the highest order and those not otherwise served can overbalance legitimate claims to the free exercise of religion."[13]

Ideally, unless the state could pass this strict scrutiny of its motives to burden a religious practice, the courts would vote in favor of those seeking exemption from the laws.

The process wasn't perfect (how, for instance, did the Court define what was "compelling" or a "paramount interest"?) and religious minorities didn't always win under it, either, especially in recent years. The Court has found reasons to infringe on certain religious practices. But the test was designed to shield the fundamental right of religious freedom from government interference.

Then came *Smith*, and overnight that protection vanished. Justice Scalia, joined by Chief Justice Rehnquist, and Justice White, Stevens, and Kennedy (O'Connor voted with the majority but refused to sign the opinion) held that the strict scrutiny test is not the appropriate standard of review for most free exercise cases. The government no longer should be burdened to prove any compelling state interest in order to justify a law that infringes upon a religious practice. Instead, if a law is not intended to interfere with a specific faith, but was a general law applying to everyone equally, then there was no constitutional right to exemption. It would be unconstitutional, for example, to make a Sunday law that specifically applied to Seventh-day Adventists, but not one that applied to everyone in general, Adventists included. If you wanted to change that law, or be exempt from it, you must go to your state legislature. If your legislature doesn't oblige, then, according to the Court—tough luck.

Scalia wrote, with four other justices agreeing, that "the record of more than a century of our free exercise jurisprudence" has made it clear that the Constitution "does not relieve an individual of the obligation to comply with a 'valid and neutral law of general applicability,'" even though the law might "incidentally" burden a religious practice.[14] For Scalia, to apply the compelling state interest test "across the board to all actions thought to be religiously commanded" would "open the prospect of constitutionally required religious exemptions of almost every conceivable kind—ranging from compulsory military service . . . to the payment of taxes . . . animal cruelty laws. . . ." To do so, he asserted, would court "anarchy."[15]

Yet the record of more than a century of free exercise jurisprudence shows that the Constitution *does* make an attempt to relieve individuals of the obligation to comply with any law that burdens their religious practice. That's the whole purpose of free exercise protection. The phrase that Congress shall make "no law" prohibiting the free exercise of religion doesn't have to mean only laws that specifically target religion (which even Scalia said were unconstitutional), but even laws of "general applicability" that would "incidentally" prohibit it. No wonder Justice Blackmun in his dissent charged that the majority decision "mischaracteriz[es] the Court's precedents" and "effectuates a wholesale overturning of settled law concerning the Religion Clauses of our Constitution."

Also, Scalia's argument that applying the compelling interest test across the board would court "anarchy" denies reality. Even after decades of applying the test, where is the anarchy? And his warning that it would require exemption from "payment of taxes" ignores a previous case in which the court—citing a compelling state interest—voted against those who, for religious reasons, didn't want to pay taxes!

Scalia cited *Minversville v. Gobitis*, a 1940 Supreme Court ruling that required Jehovah's Witness children to salute the flag, despite their religious objections to the practice. This case, considered the low point of the Court's treatment of religion, resulted in a national wave of violence against Jehovah's Witnesses. "In the two years following the *Gobitis* decision," wrote constitutional scholar Leo Pfeffer, "there was an uninterrupted record of violence and persecution of the Witnesses. Almost

without exception, the flag and flag salute were the causes."[16]
What Scalia neglected to mention, however, was that just three
years later, the Supreme Court overruled *Gobitis* and the reasoning behind it. Thus, citing *Gobitis* to justify restrictions on
religious freedom is like today quoting Joseph Stalin on the
economic glories of Communism.

No wonder Dean Kelly, counselor on religious liberty for the
National Council of Churches, said that with *Smith* the court
"virtually nullified one of the foremost guarantees of the Bill of
Rights, the Free Exercise Clause of the First Amendment."[17]
The world of post-*Smith* jurisprudence is potentially hostile to
all faiths. Citing *Smith*, a federal appeals court disallowed the
Salvation Army's religiously based claim for exemption from a
law regulating boardinghouses.[18] Citing *Smith*, a federal appeals court held valid the New York City Landmark Law, which
forbade a church from razing a structure and replacing it with
an office tower in order to gain money for its ministries.[19] And
citing *Smith*, a court turned away a prisoner's challenge to a
ban on the possession of rosaries and scapulars.[20]

If *Smith* remains as the prevailing free-exercise jurisprudence, it's not difficult to see how it could affect Adventists.
What could be a more "valid and neutral law of general applicability" than a Sunday law? Though the Sunday legislation
depicted in *The Great Controversy* is religious (as all Sunday
laws really are), it could be initiated under the veneer of economics, morality, or "family values." Indeed, in a series of cases
in the early 1960s, the Supreme Court ruled that though Sunday laws originally had a religious purpose, they were now
secular and therefore constitutional. However Sunday legislation might first come, under *Smith*, Adventists would have *no*
protection against it.

Of course, *The Great Controversy* scenario could happen only
under a reinterpretation of the Constitution far more radical
than even *Smith*. For the United States government to allow
persecution of Sabbath keepers on the pretense that their actions have "provoked the displeasure of heaven" and that only
by their punishment will this nation be restored to "divine favor
and temporal prosperity,"[21] the First Amendment would have to

be weakened into meaninglessness. That hasn't happened yet. Nevertheless, Ellen White did write that "our country shall repudiate every principle of its Constitution,"[22] and *Smith* is beyond doubt a step in that direction.

Because *Smith* was such a bad decision, Representative Stephen Solarz introduced into the House in June 1991 "A Bill to Protect the Free Exercise of Religion," H.R. 2797, otherwise known as the Religious Freedom Restoration Act. The gist of H.R. 2797 is "to restore the compelling interest test as set forth in *Sherbert v. Verner*." The bill states that the "government may burden a person's exercise of religion only if it demonstrates that application of the burden to the person—(1) is essential to further a compelling governmental interest; and (2) is the least restrictive means of furthering that compelling governmental interest."[23] In other words, if enacted into law, the bill would force the Supreme Court to restore the compelling state interest test to free exercise cases.

Unfortunately, H.R. 2797 faced many obstacles (Solarz's election defeat in September of 1992 didn't help matters either). The two days of House Committee hearings in May 1992 were an attempt to get it on track. Representing two organizations normally at each other's throats, Andrew Dugan of the National Association of Evangelicals (NAE) and Nadine Strossen of the American Civil Liberties Union (ACLU) were among those who testified in favor of passage.

"Unless Congress acts to protect religious liberty," Strossen of the ACLU testified, "the Court's ruling in *Smith* will have a devastating effect on the free exercise of religion throughout our nation. We urge quick and favorable action on H.R. 2797."[24] Dugan said that "we applaud this bipartisan bill introduced by Representative Stephen Solarz which now has more than 175 co-sponsors. H.R. 2797 would restore the balancing process which formerly prevented government from running roughshod over religious freedom. Congress must overrule the *Smith* case and restore the compelling interest test which is the heart and soul of free exercise jurisprudence."[25]

Yet H.R. 2797 met opposition, particularly among Catholics, who feared that the bill could be used as a loophole for abortion, especially if *Roe v. Wade* were overturned by the U.S. Supreme Court (it wasn't). Mark Chopko, general counsel for the United States Catholic Conference, testified before the subcommittee that H.R. 2797 "was intended to include religiously based abortion claims."[26] Chopko, along with others, pushed an alternative version, called H.R. 4040, which stipulates: "Nothing in this act shall be construed to authorize a cause of action by any person to challenge . . . any limitation or restriction on abortion, on access to abortion services or on abortion funding."[27] Proponents of the Religious Freedom Restoration Act feared that the abortion issue could stall the bill until it died, or that the amended version would never pass, killing the entire project. And that's exactly what happened. On October 5, 1992, H.R. 2797 died on the Senate side. It will be reintroduced in the 103rd Congress. Now, under Clinton, it has a much better chance of passing.

Roman Catholic opposition to H.R. 2797 adds an interesting dimension to the debate. Though *Smith* jeopardizes the free exercise of all denominations and religions, minority faiths are the most threatened. A church with many members, like the Roman Catholic, can wield enough electoral clout that no legislative body would likely pass a law placing a major burden on the free exercise rights of its adherents. The Native American Church, Amish, or Seventh-day Adventists don't have that potential. Though the Catholic Church has centered its opposition to H.R. 2797 on abortion, if, as Ellen White wrote in *The Great Controversy*, the "Roman Church is . . . employing every device to extend her influence and increase her power,"[28] the church could have ulterior motives for wanting H.R. 2797 trashed. Despite the minor hindrances to Catholics, in the long run, *Smith* could work to Rome's advantage.

Though dealing directly with free exercise, *Smith* actually symbolizes the much larger issue: What kind of government do we have? Is our country a majoritarian democracy, in which the majority rules, and decisions about rights and freedom are left to the voters? Or are we a constitutional republic, in which the government finds its power not only by popular vote, but also, as Harvard scholar Stephen Macedo wrote, by "its conformity with certain principles of justice and 'unalienable Rights,' which were held to be 'natural' or of a higher moral standing than the will of the majority"?[29] *Smith*—which places a fundamental right like free exercise of religion at the discretion of the masses—indicates that the Supreme Court is moving toward the former.

In *The Great Controversy*, Ellen White wrote that "even in free America, rulers and legislators, in order *to secure public favor*, will yield to the *popular demand* for a law enforcing Sunday observance. Liberty of conscience, which has cost so great a sacrifice, will no longer be respected."[30]

These words imply a majoritarian democracy. Our religious rights, which certainly should have "a higher moral standing than the will of the majority," will be subject to that majority anyway.

This danger is not far-fetched. The highly publicized battle over Robert Bork's nomination to the Supreme Court dealt with this basic issue. "The clash over my nomination," Bork wrote, "was simply one battle in this long running war for control of our legal culture."[31] Bork represents the majoritarians, those who would like to see more power placed in the hands of voters as opposed to the courts. For Bork, unless a right is specifically expressed in the Constitution, and interpreted according to the original intent of the framers, that right does not exist, and the courts should not invent it. "[Where] the Constitution is mute," he wrote, "we should vote about these matters rather than litigate them."[32]

That view might sound sensible, but if implemented would radically restrict our freedoms. However much Americans might revere the Constitution, it is, after all, over two hundred years old. America is a radically more complex nation now than when the Constitution was framed by the few dozen men who arrived in Philadelphia on horseback or in carriages. To interpret a two-hundred-year-old document the way the founding fathers did in a nation of less than four million people, and to suppose that this interpretation will meet all the needs, challenges, and problems of a nation two hundred years later and with sixty times the population, is expecting too much. The Constitution simply cannot be applied today the way the founding fathers would have, because they weren't dealing with our problems.

"The Constitution," wrote political satirist P. J. O'Rourke, "is an equally forthright piece of work and quite succinct—twenty-one pages (in the *American Civics* E-Z-reader large-type version) giving the complete operating instructions for a nation of 250 million people. The manual for a Toyota Camry, which seats only five, is four times as long."[33]

The problems of applying a document written in the 1780s to people living in the late 1900s can be seen in one example. Connecticut had an antiquated statute banning birth control. Law professors at Yale challenged it, and in *Griswold v. Connecticut* the Supreme Court struck the law down as an unconstitutional invasion of the "right of privacy." Wrote Justice Douglas for the majority: "Would we allow the police to search the sacred precincts of marital bedrooms for telltale signs of the use of contraceptives?"[34]

However logical Douglas's reasoning, one minor problem exists: nothing in the Constitution deals with the right of privacy, much less the use of contraceptives. Bork argued, therefore, that there is no constitutional right to either, and that the law, which he himself thought was bad, should have been invalidated—but by the state legislature, not by the courts. "There being nothing in the Constitution about maximum hours laws, minimum wage laws, contraception, or abortion," Bork wrote, "the Court should have simply said that and left the legislative decision where it was."[35]

However, Bork's reasoning is the best argument against his own conclusion. *Because* the Constitution is not specific, we need a more expansive reading to cover today's specifics. The rights and freedoms and laws in our modern society need to go beyond the literal meaning of a document that couldn't possibly address contemporary issues. What, for example, did Benjamin Franklin, George Washington, and the other framers know about airline deregulation, school busing, and wiretapping?

Also, what other rights, not mentioned in the document itself, are constitutionally protected? Do married couples have a constitutional right to make love? What about unmarried couples? What about unmarried couples of the same gender?

Because these actions aren't specifically mentioned in the Constitution, does that mean they do not exist, except by popular vote?

What makes the *Smith* decision so frightening is that it took a right *mentioned* in the document—free exercise—and placed it at the discretion of the legislative branch. If the Court can do that with rights mentioned in the Bill of Rights, what could it do with those that aren't even there?

Of course, other variables, dealing with the Ninth, Tenth, and Fourteenth Amendments, incorporation, judicial deference, states' rights, original intent, substantive due process, and at least a dozen others all figure in the debate over how the Constitution should be interpreted. What's clear, however, is that *Smith* indicates a trend toward narrowing the jurisdiction of the courts and placing more power into the hands of state and local governments.

That trend becomes even more significant because state and local government is where the New Right has been seeking power. They are its target for the nineties. Though the Supreme Court, in the Pennsylvania 1992 abortion case, didn't overturn *Roe v. Wade*, it allowed states to apply more restrictions on it, which will give the New Right even more incentive to get power at state levels in order to limit abortion as much as possible. And it's almost certain that once they gain power, they won't stop with abortion.

"Because the Supreme Court is now in the business of remanding issues to the state," warns Matthew Moen, "the New Christian Right's attempt to organize at the state level could be significant. We might be surprised to see what it will do in the 1990s."[36]

What's so important about *Smith* is that it reveals just how fragile our rights are. We like to think that the Constitution clearly and in detail enunciates our religious freedoms. Not quite. The basis of those guarantees in a nation of 250 million people and hundreds of faiths is found in only sixteen words: "Congress shall make no law respecting an establishment of religion, or prohibiting the free exercise thereof"—two very broad strokes.

"No respected church-state scholar of today," wrote Derek Davis, "is so bold as to declare, with unqualified conviction, the exact meaning of the religion clauses at the time of their passage."[37] Little agreement exists over exactly what those sixteen words mean, or the correct way to interpret them, to whom they apply, or even how to apply them. The protections they have offered have been given flesh and blood only by their interpretation in the courts. But, as *Smith* has proven, the courts can pick the bones clean.

What *Lee v. Wiseman* (the 1992 legislated-prayer-in-school case) showed, too, was that this nation was just one vote away— *one vote!*—from doing to the first ten of those words what *Smith* did to the last six—which is, all but destroy them.

Of course, now that Bill Clinton is president, he will certainly put justices on the courts more likely to protect our freedoms. The ones likely to retire, however, are those who are already sensitive to religious freedom. So, even under Clinton, the makeup of the court will still be precariously dangerous for church-state separation.

After referring to the First Amendment protections in the U.S. Constitution, Ellen White in *The Great Controversy* wrote: "Only in flagrant violation of these safeguards to the nation's liberty, can any religious observance be enforced by civil authority."[38]

With *Smith*, we've just witnessed a flagrant violation of "these safeguards to the nation's liberty."

More will come.

---

1. Quoted in Mitchell Tyner, "Is Religious Liberty a 'Luxury' We Can No Longer Afford?" *Liberty*, Sept./Oct. 1990, 5.

2. Ibid.

3. Darrell Turner, "Religious groups press to overturn decision curtailing freedoms," *Religious News Service*, 2 July 1992, 8.

4. Quoted by Ruth Marcus in "Reigns on Religious Freedom?" *Washington Post*, 9 Mar. 1991.

5. David Miller, "Religious Freedom Is Under Fire," *The Lutheran*, 17 July 1991, 8.

6. Testimony of Congressman Stephen J. Solarz Concerning the Religious Freedom Restoration Act Before the House Subcommittee on Civil and Constitutional Rights, 14 May 1992.

7. West Virginia State Board of Education v. Barnette (1943).

8. *Employment Division v. Smith* (1992).

9. *Cantwell v. Connecticut* (1946).

10. The Late Corporation of the Church of Jesus Christ of Latter Day Saints v. United States (1890).

11. Summary of Statement of Douglas Laycock Before the House Subcommittee on Civil and Constitutional Rights, 13 and 14 May 1992.

12. *Sherbert v. Verner* (1963).

13. *Wisconsin v. Yoder* (1972).

14. *Employment Division v. Smith* (1992).

15. Ibid.

16. Leo Pfeffer, *God, Caesar, and the Constitution* (Boston: Beacon Press, 1975), 144.

17. Testimony on the Religious Freedom Restoration Act presented by Dean Kelly, counselor on religious liberty to the National Council of Churches, to the subcommittee on Civil and Constitutional Rights of the Committee on the Judiciary of the House of Representatives, 13 May 1992.

18. *Salvation Army v. Department of Community Affairs.*

19. *St. Bartholomew's Church v. City of New York.*

20. *Friend v. Kolodzieczak.*

21. *The Great Controversy*, 590.

22. 5T 451.

23. H.R. 2797: To protect the free exercise of religion, 102nd Congress, 1st Session, 26 June 1991.

24. Statement of Nadine Strossen, president, and Robert S. Peck, legislative counsel, American Civil Liberties Union on H.R. 2797, The Religious Freedom Restoration Act regarding protection of religious liberty before the U.S. House Judiciary Committee Subcommittee on Civil and Constitutional Rights, 13 May 1992.

25. Statement of Robert P. Dugan, Jr., director, Office of Public Affairs, National Association of Evangelicals on H.R. 2797, the Religious Freedom Restoration Act, before the Subcommittee on Civil and Constitutional Rights of the House Committee on the Judiciary, 13 May 1992.

26. Testimony of Mark E. Chopko, general counsel on behalf of the United States Catholic Conference before the Subcommittee on Civil and Constitutional Rights of the Judiciary Committee of the United States House of Representatives on H.R. 2797, the Religious Freedom Restoration Act of 1991, 13 May 1992.

27. H.R. 4040, 102nd Congress, 1st session. Undated.

28. *The Great Controversy*, 565.

29. Stephen Macedo, *The New Right v. the Constitution* (Washington, D.C.: Cato Institute, 1987), 22.

30. *The Great Controversy*, 592, emphasis supplied.

31. Robert Bork, *The Tempting of America* (New York: Simon & Schuster, 1990), 2.

32. Ibid., 256.

33. P. J. O'Rourke, *Parliament of Whores* (New York: Vintage Books, 1991), 11.

34. *Griswold v. Connecticut* (1965).

35. Bork, 225.

36. Quoted in Clifford Goldstein, "The New Christian Right: Born Again?" *Shabbat Shalom*, April-June 1991, 6.

37. Derek Davis, *Original Intent* (Buffalo: Prometheus Books, 1991), xvi.

38. *The Great Controversy*, 442.

NINE:

The NDE Deception

I had been everywhere from Finnish Lapland to the Sea of Japan, but my strangest trip was just down the block. Not that anything particularly exciting existed there. Nothing did. But then it wasn't *where* I went that was bizarre, but *how*. I flew, right through the ceiling!

I had stretched out on my bed to nap in my rented room, a yellow wooden shack in the student ghetto of Gainesville, Florida. Soon after I closed my eyes, I felt a strange tingling in my toes that quickly moved up my body until it centered in my head. It seemed as if I were flying through a buzzing wind tunnel filled with a gray, crackling mist, like static on an empty TV station. I felt myself leave my body, rocket through the ceiling, and instantly I was floating in a mist outside the second-story apartment of two friends who lived down the block. Too scared to scream, I snapped out of it and sat up in my room, bug-eyed.

The experience enthralled me. Austrian poet Rilke once wrote, "Whoever you are: some evening take a step out of your house, which you know so well. Enormous space is near." I had taken that step. Enormous space was, indeed, near. I wanted to step out farther.

The next day I met Seventh-day Adventists in a health-food store who warned me that I was being deceived by the devil, and that what was happening to me wasn't what I thought it was. Nothing they said, however, could have convinced me that my experience was anything other than my "soul" leaving my body.

Fortunately, two days later, I had a dramatic conversion to

Jesus Christ, and those occult experiences never came back.

In early 1992, *Life* magazine ran a cover story called "Visions of Life After Death: The Ultimate Mystery," which told of those who had died and then revived. Amazingly enough, the descriptions of their Near Death Experiences (NDEs) were exactly what happened to me—except that I was nowhere near death.

"I was in a sort of a tunnel, a cloudlike enclosure," said a woman who had an NDE, "a grayish opalescence that I could practically see through. I felt wind brushing against my ears, except I didn't have ears. I was there, but my body wasn't."[1]

I know the feeling, except I didn't have to "die" to have the same experience.

Though the *Life* article said that "the popular view of near-death experiences is based largely on a view of existence that has scarcely changed in millennia: the belief that the body is inhabited by a soul or spirit or mind that informs our consciousness and leaves the body at death"[2]—in reality, NDEs—as well as my experience (called *astral travel*), are all demonic hallucinations and deceptions, twentieth-century manifestations of Satan's six thousand-year-old lie that "ye shall not surely die" (Genesis 3:4).

"The doctrine of man's consciousness in death," Ellen White warned, "especially the belief that spirits of the dead return to minister to the living, has prepared the way for modern spiritualism."[3]

The Great Controversy exudes similar warnings about modern spiritualism. She warns about spiritualism as much as she does about the Sunday law, because spiritualism is going to have a major role in Satan's final deception.

"Except those who are kept by the power of God, through faith in his word," she stated, "the whole world will be swept into the ranks of this delusion."[4]

The world's ready. All around the globe, in almost every culture, faith, and country, souls are being primed for the grand lie. Forty-two percent of Americans, for instance, believe that they have been in contact with the dead. *Forty-two percent!* If that many believe that they have contacted the dead, how many more must believe at least that the dead live on?

In 1988, *Esquire*, usually devoted to such contemplative topics as the best sushi restaurants in Manhattan or Ivana Trump's love life, ran an article by bestselling author Michael Crichton, in which he described meeting his deceased father in the astral plane.

"I hadn't had an easy time with my father. Now he was showing up while I was vulnerable, in an altered state of consciousness. I wondered what he would do, what would happen. My father looked the same, only translucent and misty, like everything else in this place. . . . Suddenly he embraced me. In the instant of the embrace, I saw and felt everything in my relationship with my father, all the feelings I had and why I had misunderstood him, all the love that was really between us, and all the confusion and misunderstanding that had overpowered it. . . . A wound that had bothered me for years had been healed."[5]

Injured during a firefight in Vietnam, Captain Tommy Clack told about leaving his body: "Around me were people I have served with who had died. They were moving away from me, communicating not with words. They were not in physical form, but I knew that was Dallas, Ralph, and Terry, and they knew me."[6]

"He [Satan] has power to bring before men the appearance of their departed friends," wrote Ellen White in *The Great Controversy*. "The counterfeit is perfect; the familiar look, the words, the tone, are reproduced with marvelous distinctness."[7]

In *Family Circle*, a woman described her NDE: "I noticed that a blue mist surrounded my body and was drifting up off the operating table."[8]

Reader's Digest described the typical phenomena: "In many cases, various auditory sensations are reported . . . a really bad buzzing noise . . . Concurrently with the noise, people often have the sensation of being pulled rapidly through a dark space of some kind. I have heard this described as a cave, a well, a trough, an enclosure, a tunnel. . . . After this passage through the tunnel, a dying person may find himself looking upon his own body from a point outside of it. . . . Words and phrases which have been used by various subjects include a mist, a cloud, a vapor, an energy pattern."[9]

McCall's said that the hundreds of stories about NDEs were "too convincing and too similar to be disbelieved."[10]

They are also similar to my occult ordeal: a loud buzzing sound, the motion through a tunnel, the sensation of being outside the body, a mist—though I didn't have to die, or even come near death, to experience them. All that was missing for me was an encounter with the "dead." No doubt, had my experiences continued, that would have happened too.

In my quest for truth, I became vulnerable to the occult,[11] and the devil—seeing my desire for spiritual experiences—gave me some, only the wrong kind. Had I not been converted to Jesus, not been truly born again within days of that experience, I would have been snared in the devil's web.

I wouldn't have been alone, either. NDEs have become almost mainstream. *Life, Esquire, Reader's Digest, McCall's*, and *Family Circle*—these aren't the *National Enquirer*. Around the world, physicians, psychologists, sociologists, biologists, and philosophers are researching NDEs. There is a *Journal of Near-Death Studies* and an International Association of Near-Death Studies. Pollsters estimate that "eight million Americans have had near-death experiences."[12]

Though similar phenomena have been recorded as far back as the *Tibetan Book of the Dead*, not until the mid-1970s—with psychiatrist Raymond Moody, Jr.'s *Life After Life*—were NDEs burned into the American psyche. Published in 1976, the book told of Moody's interviews with about fifty people who died and then revived. *Life After Life* has sold more than seven million copies and gave birth to an industry that has been growing ever since.

Years before becoming an Adventist, I read *Life After Life* in college. Though the thought pricked at me that these people weren't *dead*, like rigor-mortis-and-worms dead, I nevertheless felt an overwhelming sense of well-being, comfort, and assurance that life didn't end when our heartbeat did. Here seemed to be, if not proof, then at least powerful evidence that not only do we live after we die—and that our short, nasty little existence isn't *it*—but that we don't need to be born-again Christians to enter into the world beyond, either. Most interviewees weren't overtly religious, much less devout Christians, yet they met "God," or a powerful loving presence that talked to them in a kind, nonjudgmental, and loving manner before returning them to *terra firma*.

"Love," said Ellen White of spiritualism, "is dwelt upon as the chief attribute of God, but it is degraded to a weak sentimentalism, making little distinction between good and evil. God's justice, His denunciation of evil, the requirements of His holy law are all kept out of sight."[13]

A basic biblical doctrine is that "all have sinned and come short of the glory of God" (Romans 3:23), and that Jesus Christ is our only hope for salvation: "For there is none other name under heaven given among men, whereby we must be saved" (Acts 4:12). Yet few, if any, return from their NDE experience convicted of sin and the need for Christ's atoning blood. Though John wrote, "For this is the love of God, that we keep his commandments" (1 John 5:3), why don't those who had NDEs revive with the admonition to obey God's law? Why don't the "dead" warn about the impending judgment depicted in Scripture? Many of the contacted "dead" were never Christians to begin with, and those who reported meeting the dead rarely become committed Christians as a result of their NDE experience.

"Instead," said a *Christianity Today* article, "they tend to become suspicious of religious 'sectarianism'. . . . The modern visionaries' conversion is not to an austere spirituality, but to one that affirms joy and laughter."[14]

These facts alone should warn Christians that something isn't kosher. However, when a study by the Princeton Religion Research Center reported that a "surprising high number" of Christians identify with New Age beliefs, it's no wonder that NDEs are duping the churched as well. The Princeton study, based on a poll of 2,045 adults, said that "the line separating established religious belief and practice from superstition can be thin and indistinct."[15] One major New Age belief that a majority of Christians accepted, said the Princeton report, was "life after death."

"Many of them have seen heaven and some have been allowed to see hell . . ." wrote Pat Robertson about people who had NDEs. "For all of them, the experience has been a life-changing one, and this is a uniform testimony to the existence of life after death."[16] Though Robertson admits that these stories don't prove life after death, he claims that "they stand as support to the Bible's statement that life continues beyond the grave."[17] On the same page, Robertson says that the Bible warns against communicating with the dead, yet communicating with the "dead" is often what NDEs are all about.

Author and minister Dr. James Kennedy used Raymond Moody's NDE documentation as a witnessing tool. "You have said in the past, 'Oh, well, when somebody goes there and comes back, then I will listen.' Well, friend, start listening, because someone has been there and has been back, not merely someone, but four or five hundred different someones. . . . Every one of these people reported seeing, usually at a distance, a person whom they described as a religious 'figure.' This was true even for atheists. The Bible says there is one with whom we have to do, and that One is Jesus Christ."[18]

Kennedy didn't mention, however, that this "religious figure" never convicted them of sin, their need of repentance, and the necessity of Christ's imputed righteousness as their only hope of eternal life. Rather, after their NDE experiences, most people believe that they *have* eternal life already.

In some instances, NDEs have a more "Christian" slant. "On the twenty-first day of April 1933, Saturday night, 7:30 o'clock [sic]," wrote evangelist Kenneth Hagin, "my heart stopped beating and the spiritual man that lives in my body departed from my body. . . . Way below me, I could see lights flickering on the walls of the caverns of the damned. They were caused by the fires of hell."[19] Others talk about meeting Jesus or angels. In some cases, skeptics come back more open to spiritual things, or Christians revive renewed in their faith, but such instances do not prove NDEs are of God.

"It is true," wrote Ellen White in *The Great Controversy*, "that spiritualism is now changing its form and, veiling some of its more objectionable features, is assuming a more Christian guise."[20]

An article in *Christianity Today* took a more cautious approach to NDEs than did either Kennedy or Robertson. "If Moody's composite NDE is taken to be a revelation of life after death, it is," said the article, "in some significant respects, not what Christianity has traditionally taught."[21] For instance, though the apostle Paul viewed death as the "last enemy," the article stressed that "in contrast, the near-death visionary discovers death as an unqualified friend."[22] Though NDEs "fundamentally 'prove' nothing about life after death," the article admitted, it also said that "at best they are partial, ambiguous, fragmented, and distorted glimpses of [another world]."[23]

Christianity Today's ambivalence shows just how dangerous NDEs can be even to mature, cautious Christians who don't understand the nature of man and of death.

In a book published in 1992, *Immortality: The Other Side of Death*, two Christians use NDEs to help readers "discover what awaits you on the other side of death." Though they admit that in NDEs, "occultic elements are sometimes present," they dismiss these instances as mere "counterfeits [that] presuppose genuine ones."[24] They then list different examples of NDEs in the Bible, including Stephen's "pre-death vision," and the parable of Lazarus, because his "post-death experience has similarities with some NDEs we have discussed."[25]

In recent years a spate of books warning about the New Age have been churned out by Christians. However, no matter how many books and articles authors like Constance Cumbey, Dave Hunt, F. LaGard Smith, and others may write against Shirley MacLaine, channeling, and harmonic convergence, as long as these Christians don't know the truth about the state of the dead, all are vulnerable to the deceptions of spiritualism as well.

In an anti–New Age article in *Christianity Today*, Brooks Alexander of Spiritual Counterfeits Project said that a dominant New Age theme is the "primal lie" that "there is no death."[26] How ironic, because if Brooks Alexander believes the traditional Christian concept of the state of the dead (which he certainly does), then despite his attack on the "primal lie," he believes it himself.

After the publication of a *Liberty Alert* in which I called NDEs a "demonic hallucination,"[27] I received a strong letter from an Adventist chaplain who took me to task for making such a blanket statement. At first I thought, *Maybe I spoke too strongly*, but as I answered him, my convictions became stronger.

First, these people *all* think that their soul or spirit is leaving their body, a belief that contradicts the important biblical doctrine about the nature of man. Second, many have met the "dead" floating like disembodied spirits, another antiscriptural phenomenon. Third, few ever return convicted of their need of repentance, conversion, and faith in Jesus as their Saviour. The few who do hardly compensate for the thousands, even millions, who come back thinking they already have eternal life. And finally, NDEs are duping millions around the world with the belief that "you will not surely die."

If this isn't demonic, what is?

In an article in *Psychology Today*, psychologist and NDE researcher Ronald Siegel explains NDEs "as hallucinations, based on stored images in the brain."[28] After elaborating on the physiological factors probably involved, he wrote that "all these phenomena bear a strong resemblance to those reported in drug-induced hallucinations and in hallucinations produced by other conditions."[29] Whatever the physiological factors, NDEs are being successfully manipulated, if not directly caused, by the devil in order to dupe millions into believing that they do not die after death.

Of course, besides NDEs, the older, more "traditional" forms of spiritualism still exist. A few years ago Dr. Raymond Moody published interviews of people who claimed to have been visited by Elvis since his death in 1977. Hilda Weaver, a clinical psychologist who previously never had any interest in the paranormal, told of her encounter:

I was in my office one evening, writing an article for a professional journal, and I looked up and Elvis Presley was sitting across from me, in the comfortable tan chair where my patients usually sit. . . . I could tell that he thought all was not well with me. This was surprising because at that time I thought I was at the top of the world: a practicing psychologist, very effective, very smart. . . . He began to talk with me, to communicate. He said, "Are you satisfied with your life, Missy?" . . . Then we conversed for a while. Much of it was very personal, stuff that I'm not yet comfortable sharing with anyone else. . . . I instinctively bowed my head and put my hands together, as in prayer. When I looked up again, he was gone. And I have never seen him again. Once in a while, I play his records, and listen.[30]

"Many will be confronted," said Ellen White in *The Great Controversy*, "by the spirits of devils personating beloved relatives or friends and declaring the most dangerous heresies. These visitants will appeal to our tenderest sympathies."[31]

Meanwhile, Catholics all over the world are being swept up by the Virgin Mary deception. "A grass-roots revival of faith in the Virgin," said *Time*, "is taking place worldwide. Millions of worshippers are flocking to her shrines, many of them young people. Even more remarkable are the number of claimed sightings of the Virgin, from Yugoslavia to Colorado, in the past few years."[32]

At the same time, Protestants are being fooled by NDEs and other supernatural phenomena with a "Christian" slant. A Christian newsletter by "Mary Stewart Relfe, B.A., M.B.A., Ph.D.," told of the experience of a medical missionary in South America taken to heaven for more than five days, where he "talked with great soul winners, including Kathryn Kuhlman, Amy McPherson, and Smith Wigglesworth."[33]

And millions of others are being lulled by various New Age manifestations such as astral travel, channeling, and NDEs into a false sense of security and eternal life.

Secularist, Protestant, Catholic, Jew, Muslim, Buddhist, Hindu—because of their misunderstanding of the state of the dead, none has protection against Satan's last-day deceptions. From Billy Graham to the Dalai Lama, from the mullahs of Iran to Catholic priests in South America, all are susceptible to Satan's most subtle, powerful, and universally accepted deception that "you shall not surely die."

"Satan has long been preparing," Ellen White wrote in *The Great Controversy*, "for his final effort to deceive the world. . . . Little by little he has prepared the way for his masterpiece of deception in the development of spiritualism. He has not yet reached the full accomplishment of his designs; but it will be reached in the last remnant of time."[34]

She wrote those words more than a century ago. Spiritualism has been exponentially multiplying since. Almost the whole planet is deceived by it in one form or another. No wonder Ellen White spends so much time warning about it in *The Great Controversy*. Perhaps, with his latest manifestations of spiritualism, such as NDEs, the devil has already "reached the full accomplishment of his designs."

If not, he's close.

1. Verlyn Klinkenborg, "At the Edge of Eternity," *Life*, March 1992, 65.

2. Ibid., 73.

3. *The Great Controversy*, 551.

4. Ibid., 562.

5. Michael Crichton, "Travels With My Karma," *Esquire*, May 1988, 98.

6. Klinkenborg, 71.

7. *The Great Controversy*, 552.

8. Charles Panati, "Is There Really Life After Death?" *Family Circle*, November 1976, 78.

9. Ralph Moody, Jr., "Life After Life," *Reader's Digest*, 1 Jan. 1977, 194-215.

10. Mary Ann O'Roark, "I Have Never Again Been Afraid of Death," *McCall's*, November 1976, 96.

11. See Goldstein, *Best Seller*.

12. Klinkenborg, 66.

13. *The Great Controversy*, 558.

14. Rodney Clapp, "Rumors of Heaven," *Christianity Today*, 7 Oct. 1988, 19.

15. Quoted in *Religious News Service*, 31 Dec. 1991, 3.

16. Pat Robertson, *Pat Robertson Answers* (Nashville: Thomas Nelson, 1984), 36.

17. Ibid.

18. James Kennedy, *Evangelism Explosion* (Wheaton, Ill.: Tyndale House, 1983, 102, 103.

19. Quoted in Floyd C. McElveen, *The Beautiful Side of Death* (Grand Rapids: G. T. M., n.d.), 87.

20. *The Great Controversy*, 557, 558.

21. Clapp, 17.

22. Ibid., 18.

23. Ibid., 21.

24. Gary Habermans and J. P. Moreland, *Immortality: The Other Side of Death* (Nashville:

Thomas Nelson, 1992), 92.

25. Ibid., 93.

26. Brooks Alexander, "Theology From the Twilight Zone," *Christianity Today*, 18 Sept. 1987, 25.

27. Clifford Goldstein, "Near-Death Deceptions," *Liberty Alert*, June-July 1992, 1.

28. Ronald Siegel, "Accounting for 'Afterlife' Experiences," *Psychology Today*, January 1981, 75.

29. Siegel, 70.

30. Quoted in *Harper's*, August 1988, 34.

31. *The Great Controversy*, 560.

32. *Time*, 30 Dec. 1991, 62.

33. Mary Stewart Relfe, "Read About the Man Who Spent 5 1/2 Days in Heaven," *Relfe's Report*, no. 55, August 1984, 2.

34. *The Great Controversy*, 561.

TEN:

Satan's Consummate Deception

Despite undeniable parallels between worldwide political and religious trends and the prophecies in *The Great Controversy*, numerous, even difficult, questions remain. One of the hardest deals with the Sabbath itself. Ellen White wrote that "the Sabbath will be the great test of loyalty," and that "while the observance of the false Sabbath in compliance with the law of the state, contrary to the fourth commandment, will be an avowal of allegiance to a power that is in opposition to God, the keeping of the true Sabbath, in obedience to God's law, is an evidence of loyalty to the Creator."[1]

Of course, it's one thing to envision this scenario in the United States or other Western nations, but what about Muslim, Hindu, and Buddhist countries, where Sunday is about as holy as the Aztec god Quetzalcoatl is to High-Church Anglicans in Canterbury? How will the flag-burning fanatics in Iran who marched their children across mine fields for the glory of Allah or the Orthodox Jews in Jerusalem who stone cars that drive through their districts on the *Shabbat* or billions of other non-Christians ever be persuaded to keep Sunday holy?

We don't know. Though the Bible and the Spirit of Prophecy teach that these issues will be worldwide and that each individual will understand the issues clearly enough to make a rational choice between allegiance to God's law and allegiance to man's ("not one is made to suffer the wrath of God," she wrote, "until the truth has been brought home to his mind and conscience, and has been rejected"[2])—how all nations will be caught

113

up in the final events has not been revealed. The following is one possible scenario.

In the last days of Jesus' earthly ministry, He warned about false christs. "Then if any man shall say unto you, Lo, here is Christ, or there; believe it not. For there shall arise false Christs, and false prophets, and shall shew great signs and wonders; insomuch that, if it were possible, they shall deceive the very elect" (Matthew 24:23, 24).

Ellen White, in *The Great Controversy*, describes how Satan himself will appear as the consummate false christ. "As the crowning act in the great drama of deception, Satan himself will personate Christ. . . . In different parts of the earth, Satan will manifest himself among men as a majestic being of dazzling brightness, resembling the description of the Son of God given by John in the Revelation. Revelation 1:13-15. The glory that surrounds him is unsurpassed by anything that mortal eyes have yet beheld."[3]

Though this deception could dupe Christians, what about Muslims in the Sahara, Jews in Galilee, or Buddhists in the Himalayas? How could Satan's "crowning act" affect them?

A possible answer lies in the eschatology of these other faiths. Christians are not the only ones expecting a Saviour. Jews, Buddhists, Hindus, and Muslims all anticipate the arrival of a supernatural personage, a future deliverer, who will arise after a period of upheaval and bring peace and happiness to the world. It's this universal hope of an end-time divine deliverer that could open the rest of the world to Satan's consummate deception.

Take the Jews. "All the prophets prophesied," says the Talmud, "only for messianic times." The great Jewish philosopher Moses ben Maimonides (1135-1204) taught that the coming of the Messiah was a basic Jewish belief, and in the twelfth of his thirteen Articles of Faith, he stated: "I firmly believe in the coming of the Messiah; and although He may tarry, I daily hope for His coming." Despite great confusion about the Messiah's advent, many believed, and still do, that He would appear during a time of great trouble, called the "Messianic Woes," when He would rescue His people and usher in a millennium of peace.

Bar Kokba, Serene of Syria, Obayah Abu-Isa ben Ishak, David Alroy, Solomon Molcho, Abraham Abulafia, Isaac Luria, Shabbetai Zebi, Jacob Frank, and others all made messianic declarations—and through the centuries thousands have believed them, often with disastrous results.

Even today a feverish messianism pulses among some Orthodox Jews. Many believe that the Lubavitcher Rebbe in Brooklyn, Menachem Schnerrson, will reveal himself as the Messiah. A few years ago zealots in Israel tried to blow up the Dome of the Rock in Jerusalem. Their motive was to enrage the Arabs, who would wage such a vicious jihad against Israel that "the Messiah would come to save his people from destruction."

The Muslims, meanwhile, not only believe in a divine "Restorer of the Faith," but many associate him with the returned Jesus. The Koran makes reference to Christ's second coming (IV, 159). Known in Islamic tradition as the Mahdi, the twelfth in a line of Imams, the "Rightly Guided One" will usher in a thousand years of peace and justice after ending the reign of "antichrist." According to one Islamic tradition, the antichrist will devastate the whole world, leaving only Mecca and Medina in security, as these holy cities will be guarded by angelic legions. Christ at last will descend to earth and in a great battle will destroy the "man-devil."

Though all orthodox Muslims believe in the return of a divine "Restorer," they disagree on the exact nature of the return, a situation that has bred bogus Mahdis. Among them was Muhammad Ahmad, the Mahdi of Sudan, who revolted against the Egyptian administration in 1881 and after several spectacular victories established a theocratic state that lasted until 1898, when the British conquered it. Mirza Ghulam Ahmad, claiming to be the Mahdi, gained a following in the 1800s. Ali Mohammed of Shiraz declared: "I am, I am the promised one. . . . I am the one whose name you have for a thousand years invoked, at whose mention you have risen, whose advent you have longed to witness." He was shot by a firing squad. His sect exists today, known as the Baha'i.

According to Hindu belief, the god Vishnu incarnates himself whenever evil prevails. The most important incarnation, however, will be in the form of Kalki, who will appear in the clouds with a flaming sword in his hand, riding on a white steed. He will destroy all evildoers in an apocalyptic battle that will initiate a thousand-year reign of peace on the earth.

So similar is this expectation to the Christian messianic hope that years ago a missionary to India wrote a tract showing that the true deliverer and king of righteousness had already come in the person of Jesus Christ. So striking seemed the fulfillment from a Hindu perspective that hundreds in the city of Rampore accepted Christ as an incarnation of Vishnu.

According to some Buddhist sects, a long procession of bodhisattvas as incarnations of Buddha has appeared on the earth to bestow knowledge upon mankind. In some sects a future saviour, the last Buddha, called Maitreya, "Son of Love," is expected to appear from heaven and bring great spiritual blessings. Though there is little incentive in Buddhism for any would-be messiahs, in Japan in 1910 a journalist appeared on the streets of Tokyo and claimed to be the Messiah-Buddha, asserting that he was the "consummation of all the prophecies since the beginning of the world." He and his small movement eventually faded away.

And ever since Jesus said, "Behold, I come quickly," Christians have been anticipating His return. Though the Bible, especially the New Testament, teems with advent texts, Christians disagree on when He will come, where He will come, how He will come, and what He will do when He does.

This advent hope, coupled with the confusion over the particulars, has nurtured countless false christs. In 1534 radical Anabaptist John of Leiden declared himself a messianic king and took over the city of Münster in Westphalia. James Nayler, a seventeenth-century Quaker leader in England, had a large following who believed he was the messiah. In Russia messianic movements started under several false messiahs, including the notorious Skoptsy sect of the 1700s, whose leader demanded that his male followers be castrated. In China a self-proclaimed messiah, Hung Hsiu-Ch'üan, initiated a rebellion that took twenty million lives between 1850 and 1864. In America William E. Riker claimed he was the Holy Spirit and in the 1940s founded Holy City, California—his New Jerusalem.

Even today, false christs abound. Sun Myung Moon's messianic claims have received much publicity. Jesus Christ Lightning Amen, a middle-aged recluse reported to be living somewhere in the Arizona desert, gets less publicity but nonetheless has a following.

The world's great religions have at least two important similarities that could become factors in Satan's grand deception: all expect a divine personage to appear and usher in an era of peace, and all have discord within their own faith about the nature of this appearing.

In *The Great Controversy* Ellen White describes the chaos prior to the second coming. She quotes Revelation 12:12: "Woe to the inhabiters of the earth and of the sea! for the devil is come down unto you, having great wrath, because he knoweth that he hath but a short time." She places this verse in the last days: "Fearful are the scenes," she writes, "which call forth this exclamation from the heavenly voice. The wrath of Satan increases as his time grows short, and his work of deceit and destruction will reach its culmination in the time of trouble."[4]

Historically, messianic fervor among the different faiths climaxed during crisis times because the people saw a divine deliverer as their only hope. Imagine, then, the messianic expectation of Hindus, Jews, Muslims, Christians, even Buddhists as they face "a time of trouble, such as never was since there was a nation even to that same time" (Daniel 12:1), especially since most expect the messiah to come during a time of trouble anyway.

Then, in the midst of this great turmoil, Satan will appear "in different parts of the earth" in unsurpassed glory. He comes—"a majestic being of dazzling brightness"—to the Islamic world in the way Mahdi is expected, and Muslims bow down on their prayer carpets before the "Rightly Guided One," who will usher in the thousand years of peace. In glory unsurpassed by anything that "mortal eyes have yet beheld," he arrives among the Hindus, who see him as Kalki, the final and climactic incarnation of Vishnu. The Jews rejoice; their long-awaited *Moshiach* has finally arrived, not as a humble servant but as a powerful supernatural king who will end the "Messianic Woes." The Buddhists see Maitreya, come to bestow blessing upon mankind. And as Ellen White wrote, Christians at his appearing shout, " 'Christ has come! Christ has come!' "[5] And New Agers see him as all of these divine personages in one!

All these groups—confused about the nature of the advent to begin with—have been duped in the past by charlatans with much less deceptive power than the devil himself. If thousands can today believe that convicted tax cheat Sun Myung Moon is the returned Christ, what will happen when Satan himself in "unsurpassed" glory makes the claim?

Also, if a divine personage—a false Jesus, Kalki, or Maitreya, it doesn't matter which—appeared on the earth, it wouldn't take long for millions in the few last bastions of Communism to realize just how unreal "socialist realism" is.

Satan, impersonating Christ, speaks deep truths, heals the sick, and performs other miracles. In the Muslim world he quotes from the Koran, and before Christians "he presents some of the same gracious, heavenly truths which the Saviour uttered."[6] Then, because the world is suffering in a terrible time of trouble, he tells the non-Christians that to help end the woes they all should have a common day, Sunday, to worship God. In this "strong, almost overmastering delusion" he makes the same appeal to the Christian world, claiming "to have changed the Sabbath to Sunday."[7]

And the billions of the world—desperate for the wars, the earthquakes, the famines, the pestilence, and the violence to end—obey the words of their long-awaited deliverer and pay homage to the false Sabbath, thus receiving the mark of the beast.

Speculation? Of course. But can it be coincidence that the world's great religions all expect a divine personage to usher in an era of peace? Will Satan orchestrate his paramount subterfuge by fulfilling mankind's distorted expectations?

He certainly seems to be preparing the world for it now. A few years ago various New Age groups spent hundreds of thousands of dollars advertising in the world's foremost newspapers that the Messiah of the Jews, the Mahdi of the Muslims, the Christ of Christians, the Maitreya of Buddhists, and the Krishna of the Hindus were all names for one individual and that he would bring peace to the world. In October of 1986 the pope brought together 150 religious leaders from a dozen faiths—everyone from the Archbishop of Canterbury to the Dalai Lama—to pray for world peace.

Yet peace hasn't come, and won't. And, as the earth descends into the time of trouble such as never was, billions will plead for Maitreya, Kalki, the Messiah, the Mahdi, or Jesus to come. Then, as Satan executes his grandest lie, he just might appear to each religion as the peace bringer for whom they have long been waiting, words of love flowing from his lips—words that delude everyone.

Or, almost everyone.

"Only those who have been diligent students of the Scriptures," wrote Ellen White, "and who have received the love of the truth will be shielded from the powerful delusion that takes the world captive."[8]

---

1. *The Great Controversy*, 605.
2. Ibid.
3. Ibid., 624.
4. Ibid., 623.
5. Ibid., 624.
6. Ibid.
7. Ibid.
8. Ibid., 625.

ELEVEN:

Trends

L ast year an Adventist visiting my office at the General Conference said, *"The Great Controversy's* message was relevant for Ellen White's time, but outdated for ours."

Though I politely disagreed, I should have taken out the *Time* ("The Holy Alliance") issue, pushed it into his face, and replied, "Wake up now—or you will be in the second resurrection!"

Outdated? Had he said that some material, language, and references were, I would agree. If Ellen White were writing *The Great Controversy* today, she'd be quoting from Pat Robertson and Archbishop Runcie, not from Charles Beecher. She'd use words other than *Romanists, papists,* and *popery,* which now sound archaic. She'd talk about astral projections, NDEs, and channeling, rather than about spiritualism in general. In that sense, yes, the book could be considered outdated—*but to say that its basic thrust belongs to her time, not ours . . . ?*

Over the years, Adventists have made numerous false predictions about prophecy, and these mistakes have hardened some to our eschatology. Turkey, we were assured, would have a major role in last-day events. World War I was the beginning of the end. World War II was Armageddon. The "kings of the east" in Revelation was Hirohito's army. The Jews would *never* have a homeland again in Palestine. President John F. Kennedy would bring the national Sunday law.

The problem: we were too specific, when prophecy, either biblical or extra-biblical, isn't. *The Great Controversy*, for instance, covers the era from Christ's death to the new earth, all in less than seven hundred pages (the book of Revelation does it in twenty-five). A trained historian couldn't do the Reformation justice in that space, much less the entire Christian epoch and beyond. The book isn't a detailed history of Christianity; rather, *The Great Controversy* surveys the "principles"[1] behind the battle between Christ and Satan. It does not deal with specifics.

Thus, specific world events in and of themselves shouldn't become the obsessive focus of prophecy; rather, they should be analyzed only as part of the larger prophetic trends. Locking ourselves dogmatically onto specific political events, such as the JFK presidency, is dangerous. In that case, what was important wasn't so much Kennedy himself, or what he might do as president, but what it revealed about growing Catholic influence in America. Beyond that, his presidency was prophetically meaningless.

In the previous chapters, I have tried to show how *trends* match what was written in *The Great Controversy*. The details become relevant only as they fit the big picture. Individual events in and of themselves should *not* be our dominant focus.

Ellen White, for example, in the context of the churches uniting on common points of doctrine in order to enforce Sunday worship, quoted in *The Great Controversy* an excerpt from an 1846 sermon by Protestant leader Charles Beecher, in which he said: "And what do we see just ahead? Another general council! A world's convention! Evangelical alliance, and universal creed!"[2] There was, however, no universal creed or evangelical alliance "just ahead." Today, in the scheme of things, his words have become outdated, irrelevant, and insignificant. But the trend they dealt with, the uniting of the churches, was significant—even if it didn't happen at the time or in the way Beecher expected.

What's important, for example, about *The Keys of This Blood* is not the book itself, or even its details, but the trends it represents. Even Pope John Paul II himself isn't crucial. He's over seventy: The man's been shot, and last year he had a tumor removed from his colon. He could be dead in a year. What's crucial is not John Paul II as a person, or even his specific pontificate, but the direction that he has moved his church and its growing international prestige.

Reagan and the pope, working in a clandestine operation to support Solidarity, weren't depicted in the pages of prophecy—but the trend their actions symbolized was.

In the 1980s Jerry Falwell's Moral Majority fit prophecy perfectly. Today, it's history. Moral Majority, in and of itself, wasn't prophetic. The trend behind it was.

In the 1990s we have Pat Robertson and the Christian Coalition. Five years from now, Christian Coalition could go the way of Moral Majority, and Robertson the way of Jimmy Bakker. It's the trend that counts.

Look at them: the collapse of Communism, the rise of the papacy as a powerful geopolitical entity, the United States as the world's only superpower, burgeoning spiritualism, the New Right, the unity of Catholics and Protestants. Any one of these trends by itself would be significant enough, but all happening simultaneously give incredible credence not only to *The Great Controversy*, but to the whole Adventist message.

Of course, prophecy can be misused, which is another reason why many Adventists have erred. Jesus described the purpose of prophecy when He said, "And now I have told you before it comes, that when it does come to pass, you may believe" (John 14:29, NKJV). Prophecy isn't to make us clairvoyants who boldly predict the future; rather, it's to strengthen our faith when the prophecies come to pass. And, *if the prophetic trends over the past few years haven't strengthened our faith—nothing will*.

Nevertheless, attacks within Adventism against the Spirit of Prophecy continue. Some harp on the "plagiarism" issue. Others claim to have rediscovered the "gospel," which they misinterpret in a way that negates *The Great Controversy's* explanation of the investigative judgment. They're singing and hoofing to the same tired old song and dance. They need a new score.

A new score *has* been written, by those who—while professing great admiration for *The Great Controversy*—point out all its "errors" and offer their own date-setting "solutions" and reinterpretations that in reality can only undermine faith in the entire message.

No question, the devil hates *The Great Controversy*, and he is using those from both the extreme left and the extreme right to weaken our faith in it. Why? Not simply because the book exposes his wiles, but because from the first chapter, where Ellen White describes Christ weeping for Israel, to the last, where Jesus lives with His redeemed in the world made new—every page is drenched in the blood of our Redeemer. From its account of the early church, the papal darkness, the Reformation, the Millerite movement, the final crisis, the millennium, and her description of all "the years of eternity, as they roll, [that] will bring richer and still more glorious revelations of God and of Christ,"[3] this book reveals the cross of Calvary and the salvation Jesus has wrought out for every human being who accepts it.

Indeed, the most powerful aspect of *The Great Controversy* is not its prophetic message, but its spiritual one. Much more than a warning about coming persecution, Sunday laws, and the end of the world, the book is a modern revelation of Christ's love for us and His efforts to save us from ourselves. The mere existence of the book itself bears irrefutable witness to God's love, much more the powerful revelation of Christ within its pages.

"We cannot know," she wrote, "how much we owe to Christ for the peace and protection which we enjoy. It is the restraining power of God that prevents mankind from passing fully under the control of Satan."[4]

"Heavenly angels," she wrote, "had seen the glory which the Son of God shared with the Father before the world was, and they had looked forward with intense interest to His appearing on Earth as an event fraught with the greatest joy to all people. . . . Christ had stooped to take upon Himself man's nature; He was to bear an infinite weight of woe as He should make His soul an offering for sin."[5]

"We may go to Jesus and be cleansed, and stand before the law without shame or remorse."[6]

"While Jesus is pleading for the subjects of His grace, Satan accuses them before God as transgressors. . . . Jesus does not excuse their sins, but shows their penitence and faith, and, claiming for them forgiveness, He lifts His wounded hands before the Father and the holy angels, saying, I know them by name. I have graven them on the palms of My hands."[7]

"Our precious Saviour invites us to join ourselves to Him, to unite our weakness to His strength, our ignorance to His wisdom, our unworthiness to His merits. God's providence is the school in which we are to learn the meekness and lowliness of Jesus."[8]

"One reminder [of sin] alone remains: Our Redeemer will ever bear the marks of His crucifixion. Upon His wounded head, upon His side, His hands and feet, are the only traces of the cruel work that sin has wrought."[9]

"The cross of Christ will be the science and the song of the redeemed through all eternity. In Christ glorified they will behold Christ crucified. Never will it be forgotten that He whose power created and upheld the unnumbered worlds through the vast realms of space, the Beloved of God, the Majesty of heaven, He whom cherub and shining seraph delighted to adore— humbled Himself to uplift fallen man; that He bore the guilt and shame of sin, and the hiding of His Father's face, till the woes of a lost world broke His heart and crushed out His life on Calvary's cross. That the Maker of all worlds, the Arbiter of all destinies, should lay aside His glory and humiliate Himself from love to man will ever excite the wonder and adoration of the universe. As the nations of the saved look upon their Redeemer and behold the eternal glory of the Father shining in His countenance; as they behold His throne, which is from everlasting to everlasting, and know that His kingdom is to have no end, they break forth in rapturous song: 'Worthy, worthy is the Lamb that was slain, and hath redeemed us to God by His own most precious blood!'"[10]

Also, by bearing witness to the saints who through the ages loved Christ so much that they faced the dungeon, the rack, and the stake for their Saviour, *The Great Controversy* reveals the poverty of our own relationship to Jesus. These heroes of faith could do what they did only out of love for Christ. We need the same. *The Great Controversy*, by pointing us to Jesus, can, under the influence of the Holy Spirit, kindle in us a love for Jesus that persists in the face of fervent, unrelenting opposition.

Those who prayerfully read *The Great Controversy* will be led to the book behind it: the Bible—and those grounded in the Bible will not be deceived by the deceptions duping the world. "So closely will the counterfeit resemble the truth," she wrote about Satan's final deception, "that it will be impossible to distinguish between them except by the Holy Scriptures."[11]

And, finally, *The Great Controversy* screams of the nearness of Christ's coming. *Sure, we've heard all this before. Jesus' coming has been near for the past one hundred years.* Yet never in the past one hundred years have world events dovetailed as they do now. Never have the pieces fallen so precisely into place. There were always major portions that didn't fit: the Soviet Union, American anti-Catholicism, spreading Communism, strong First Amendment protections—whatever. None of these are obstacles any longer.

We don't know dates or times. We're not supposed to. In condemnation of those who date everything from the latter rain to the close of probation and the Sunday law, Ellen White warns: "Let all our brethren and sisters beware of anyone who would set a time for the Lord to fulfill His word in regard to His coming, or *in regard to any other promise He has made of special significance.*"[12]

We might not know dates, but we should be able to read the signs of the times, and those who take historic Adventism seriously have to be excited at what they portend. Jesus is coming to take us home, and we have more evidence of that promise now than ever. We must believe, trust, and obey as if our eternal destiny depended on it—because it does. We've come too far to turn back now.

As Adventists, we have been given all the reasons in the world, and even beyond, to trust the Spirit of Prophecy. The attacks against *The Great Controversy*, the indifference toward it, the growing skepticism about it—also are all trends that we have been warned about beforehand, and these also should increase our faith. Ellen White, interpreting the Bible through the lens of her prophetic gift, has more than validated that gift, and nowhere is that validation more clear and irrefutable than in *The Great Controversy*.

Nevertheless, be prepared: *The Great Controversy* embarrassment is coming. We will look like fools, idiots, and buffoons before the world—especially because of this book, which will incite those who reject the truths in it just as it incites Adventists who reject those truths even now. Indeed, how Adventists react to *The Great Controversy* today probably reveals how they will react then—only worse. Either we will surrender unconditionally to the Holy Spirit, and *The Great Controversy* will draw us closer into the embrace of Christ, who inspired its words and who has sealed each page with His blood; or, rejecting the Spirit, we will be lured into the clutches of the one who spilled Christ's blood and seeks ours as well.

"And the dragon was wroth with the woman, and went to make war with the remnant of her seed, which keep the commandments of God and have *the testimony of Jesus Christ*" (Revelation 12:17).

"For the testimony of Jesus *is the spirit of prophecy*" (Revelation 19:10).

Italics, definitely, supplied.

---

1. *The Great Controversy*, xii.
2. Quoted in ibid., 445.
3. Ibid., 678.
4. Ibid., 36.
5. Ibid., 313.
6. Ibid., 477.
7. Ibid., 484.
8. Ibid., 623.
9. Ibid., 674.
10. Ibid., 651, 652.
11. Ibid., 593.
12. Ellen G. White, *Testimonies to Ministers* (Mountain View, Calif.: Pacific Press, 1962), 55, emphasis supplied.